Deer

Animal
Series editor: Jonathan Burt

Deer

John Fletcher

REAKTION BOOKS

To Roger Short, who started me off

Published by
REAKTION BOOKS LTD
33 Great Sutton Street
London EC1V ODX, UK
www.reaktionbooks.co.uk

First published 2014
Copyright © John Fletcher 2014

Printed and bound in China by C&C Offset Printing Co., Ltd

A catalogue record for this book is available from the British Library

ISBN 9 781 78023 088 7

Contents

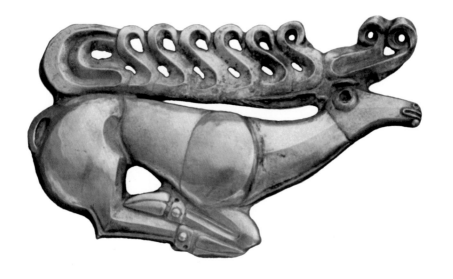

Introduction

This book is designed to appeal to both the scientifically literate as well as to those with a background in the arts. Society has never been more culturally divided between those with a scientific education and those without, and yet, ironically, there has never been a greater or more urgent need for cross-fertilization between science and the arts. Deer are ideal ambassadors to contribute, in a small way, to the breaking down of those frontiers.

Originating in the boreal regions, deer are the northern temperate grazing and browsing animals par excellence. They are supremely adapted to the seasonal availability of vegetation, as witnessed by the deciduous nature of their antlers, which are cast and regrown annually like leaves on a tree. This has made them especially fascinating not only to scientists but to myth-makers from prehistory to the present, who have used them as symbols of regeneration and longevity.

With the exception of the reindeer, until recently deer had never been domesticated. Thus, unlike the exploited and down-trodden livestock, they preserved their mystery. The domestic bovids – cattle, sheep and goats – with which we are more familiar, bear horns that are retained throughout the animal's life. They are less seasonal, originating for the most part in the southern temperate regions of the Middle East. Eurasians's connection and even dependence on deer is much more ancient

Scythian gold stag, c. 400–300 BC.

than the domestication of livestock, for in almost all cultures throughout prehistory, deer, especially, within Eurasia, red deer, were the preferred objects of the hunt.

Deer furnished antlers. The earliest sign of human life, over two million years ago, is identifiable by stone tools and for at least half a million years the antlers from deer, where available, provided our best means of knapping flints into useful shapes. In addition, by a strange symmetry, antlers provided tips for the arrows and spears with which deer were killed.

The history of humankind's adventure on this planet has been dominated thus far by the success of people from the temperate regions in making technological advances and then colonizing the rest of humanity, often brutally. In this journey deer have been our cultural companions from the snake-eating stags of Hesiod to Bambi and Rudolph.

There is now a pressing need for deer to be understood broadly, from all disciplines. As we hunt less, instead using livestock for meat, deer numbers grow. Increasingly we share their physical space as they become more suburban and mankind becomes more populous. We are compelled to make decisions that will affect them. If they become too numerous, they not only damage our forests, farms and gardens but prevent trees regenerating and destroy wild flowers and the habitats of nesting birds. Within Europe, collisions between cars and deer injure around 30,000 people annually and result in around 150 fatalities. The figures from North America are similar. The deer suffer too: almost 1 million deer are killed annually on European roads and 1.5 million in the USA. And if deer populations become too dense, suffering and mortality through starvation and disease increase. Should we stand by and allow that, or take an active role in controlling deer numbers? There are no quick fixes here. Contraception is still no panacea – there are many welfare implications in administering drugs and in coping with ageing deer too.

To make intelligent decisions about the management of deer, we need to be informed both scientifically and culturally. We must examine deer from historical, biological and cultural viewpoints. We cannot risk these mysterious, fleetingly glimpsed, symbolically charged animals being degraded to the status of vermin or sentimentalized in a brainless anthropomorphic way. At the moment, the only feasible means of management lies in hunting, yet most Western countries are experiencing a growing shortage of hunters.

In our overwhelmingly city-based society, in which even those who live in the country are in many respects urbanized, the value of hunting is not understood. As a means of approaching and comprehending nature, of spiritual renewal, of coming closer to the animals and of taking pride in their humane treatment, hunting still has a vital role. The crosscultural approach of this book permits us to place deer in their context as a family but also to examine the place deer have held in history, largely through their crucial role as quarry in hunting.

From the prehistoric societies that moved deer to offshore islands, through the exploitation of reindeer in arctic Asia and the amazing 3,000 or more medieval deer parks in England, right up to today's 1.5 million domesticated red deer on New Zealand deer farms, this book will link mankind with deer. But it will be against a background of the evolution of the many species within the deer family, an understanding of their survival strategies, and the myth and symbolism they have inspired.

1 The Family of Deer

The English word 'deer' strictly encompasses the entire tribe of mammals belonging to the family Cervidae. But it was not always so. Originally the Old English *dior* or Norse *djur* was even more inclusive, probably deriving from *dhus*, meaning 'to breathe', and so being attached to all living things other than plants. That such an important general word became so specific is an indication of the importance attached to deer at a time when European languages were evolving. In many European languages a word similar to our word *deer* is applied to all animals, as in the German *Tier*.

In this book I will use 'deer' to denote all the members of the Cervidae family. This is scientifically correct, but it is worth pointing out that in North America only the white-tailed, black-tailed and mule deer are commonly described as deer, while the moose and caribou, and even the elk or wapiti, are often excluded. That is despite the fact that the moose and the wapiti, individuals of which species often weigh half a ton, are the largest of all Cervidae and all three proudly carry the antlers that are the most visible characteristic of deer.

The 40 accepted species of the family Cervidae are herbivores and fit into the huge group loosely termed the ungulates or hoofed mammals.[1] This group in turn is divided into the odd-toed or Perissodactyls, comprising the horses, tapirs and

Mule deer buck.

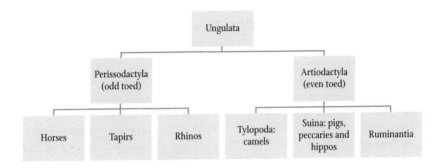

```
                          Ungulata
            ┌────────────────┴────────────────┐
      Perissodactyla                     Artiodactyla
       (odd toed)                         (even toed)
    ┌───────┼───────┐           ┌──────────┼──────────┐
  Horses  Tapirs  Rhinos   Tylopoda:   Suina: pigs,  Ruminantia
                            camels      peccaries and
                                        hippos
```

Figure 1 The Ungulates or hoofed mammals.

rhinoceroses, and the much larger genus of the even-toed or Artiodactyls, the cloven-hoofed animals (figure 1).

From recent techniques of gene analysis we now know that, bizarrely, the Artiodactyls are closely related to the whales and dolphins or Cetaceans. Some scholars have even suggested that they should form a single group, the Cetartiodactyls. This order would include not only whales but also camels, pigs and the massive sub-order of ruminants that is subdivided into the Tragulids – the mouse-deer or chevrotains – and the infra-order comprising the vast majority of ruminants, namely the horned ruminants or Pecora.

It is among the Pecora that we find the Cervidae, together with four other families: the musk deer, which are not deer at all; the Bovidae, including cattle, sheep, goats, gazelles and antelope; the giraffes, to which family deer are probably most closely related; and the pronghorns (figure 2). Among the Artiodactyla, the Bovids can claim the most species, but not far behind them come the Cervids, with 40.

For many years it was assumed that the most 'primitive' extant deer were the musk deer. Yet despite their common name, they are now recognized as being a separate family, differing from deer in having no antlers; female musk deer have only two

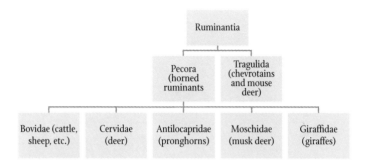

Ruminantia

Pecora (horned ruminants

Tragulida (chevrotains and mouse deer)

Bovidae (cattle, sheep, etc.)

Cervidae (deer)

Antilocapridae (pronghorns)

Moschidae (musk deer)

Giraffidae (giraffes)

teats while deer have four; their young are not spotted; and they have gall bladders. Nobody knows why, but true deer do not have gall bladders, so if you are watching someone, usually the hapless veterinarian, doing a deer autopsy, just try asking them to point out the gall bladder. For these and other reasons, musk deer are now no longer considered to be deer. Nevertheless, despite the misnomer, they deserve a mention: for from a scent gland known as the musk sac or 'pod', situated between the penis and the umbilicus, the male produces what has been notoriously the most expensive animal product, musk. The trade in musk is at least 2,500 years old and probably much older. It was until recently a key component in the perfume industry but most is now used in Chinese traditional medicine. Each male when killed yields only about 25 g of musk but at a reported value that was once four times that of gold, this is sufficient reward to stimulate widespread snaring and trapping. All species of the genus are now threatened. In China efforts to farm the musk deer so that they can be repeatedly 'milked' may reduce the killing of wild musk deer but this may come at a cost to the welfare of the captive animals.

Deer are conspicuously characterized by their antlers, which, like leaves on a tree, are deciduous: that is, they fall off and

Figure 2 The Ruminants.

Harrison's Musk Cologne, prepared in Philadelphia. All species of musk deer (which are not actually members of the deer family) are today endangered by poachers.

regrow. Thus they are very different from the horns of the bovids, which show incremental growth throughout their life. It is possible, for example, to age a goat by counting the rings around his horn, because the horns grow faster in the abundant warm days of summer than in the cold hungry winter, the rings corresponding to the periods of slow growth.

In 1878 an Anglo-Irish Ulsterman, Sir Victor Brooke, published a remarkable 40-page paper in the *Proceedings of the Zoological Society of London* entitled 'On the Classification of the Cervidae, with a Synopsis of the Existing Species'.[2] He was an improbable author: an archetypal Victorian aristocrat, sportsman, mountaineer and big game hunter who carried out amazing feats of weightlifting, wrestling and high-jumping. Later in life he became a founder committee member of the All England Lawn Tennis Association at Wimbledon and, in France, a master of the Pau Foxhounds, stocking the region with over 70 vixens and importing Irish horses and English hounds. Having lost his father when he was ten, Brooke never went to university and from the age of twenty-one he managed the 35,000 acre family estate, Colebrooke in Co. Fermanagh, with its 900 tenants and two deer parks that had been stocked with fallow deer since the time of James I. In fact on his twenty-first birthday he was enjoying his third big game hunting expedition to India.

Brooke died in 1891 at only 48 years of age, but he was no ordinary Victorian sportsman: with extraordinary single-mindedness he devoted the ten years between 1870 and 1880 to studying and publishing on the horned and antlered animals that he stalked and killed in India and Europe. To modern minds, serious zoology and big game hunting may seem incompatible but Brooke had no such qualms; those worries belonged to another century. He attended lectures in London at the Royal College of Surgeons, teaching himself French, German and Italian so as to be able to read scientific literature published abroad. Apparently easily absorbing Darwin's theories, he was able to converse and discuss his ideas with Professor Thomas Henry Huxley, Sir William Flower, Louis Agassiz and other eminent zoologists. He even conducted experiments and reported the effects of castrating deer on antler growth.

Brooke's familiarity with the habits and appearance of his quarry must have helped him, but it was his painstaking anatomical analysis of the bones of the deer that led him to propose a basic division of the Cervidae family into two groups based on the position of the splint bones in the lower limbs. Rather esoterically for the lay person, on the basis of this anatomical nicety, he classed deer as either telemetacarpalian – having the second and fifth metacarpals, the shin bones, reduced to splints at the foot end of the leg – or plesiometacarpalian, with those metacarpals reduced to splints at the upper end.

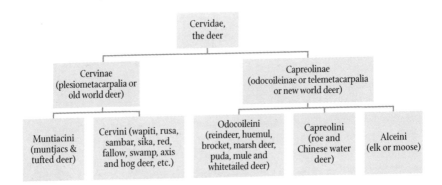

Figure 3 The Cervidae family.

Like all attempts to classify the deer, Brooke's taxonomic classification has been subjected to criticism and amendment ever since it was first published in 1878, but now, with the application of the modern tools of DNA analysis in the field of molecular phylogenetics, Brooke has been entirely vindicated. It is an amazing example of what the careful and logical field naturalist can achieve, and a credit to a remarkable Victorian polymath.

Like most groups of mammals, the primordial ruminants probably began to evolve in the cauldron of tropical climates of the Eocene, about 40 million years ago. But it was not until the Miocene, probably less than ten million years ago, that the family of Cervidae separated from the Bovidae, both groups having previously diverged from the giraffes and pronghorn antelopes.[3]

The primitive deer lived in tropical woodland or open country, not dense forest, in either eastern Eurasia or India. It had three-point antlers with a brow point and a simple fork, a long tail, little or no rump patch and a short mane. It was spotted, certainly while young, and had canine teeth and deep face glands. The male roared but did not hold harems and was only around 35 per cent larger than the female.

Approximately eight million years ago, the Cervinae and Capreolinae sub-families, corresponding respectively to Sir Victor Brooke's plesiometacarpalians, the Old World deer, and telemetacarpalians, the New World deer, diverged within the family Cervidae. One or two million years later, as the Miocene became the Pliocene, five tribes of deer surfaced: within the Cervinae, the Muntjacs diverged from the Cervini tribe and within the Capreolinae, the Alceini tribe (that is, the elk or moose) appeared; then the roe deer, the Capreolini tribe, emerged and the Odocoileini diverged (figure 3). It was during the Pliocene, between around five and two million years ago, that most of the genera of deer appeared, and during the Pleistocene that the plethora of species we now recognize evolved.

The uplift of the Tibetan plateau began around eleven million years ago and continued for 3.5 million years, and it seems most likely that the divergence of the deer family into its five tribes took place in Central Asia during the closing stages of this event. Globally there was an increase in drier and more seasonal climates with an associated spread of grasslands, and many other ruminant groups such as the sheep and goats, the buffalo and some antelope groups also emerged at this time.[4]

THE OLD WORLD DEER

Recent attempts to classify the Old World deer by analysing their genes have argued for the division of the group into two: the muntjacs, including the tufted deer, and then the very large and important Cervini (figure 4).[5] The latter group includes the barasingha or swamp deer and the spotted deer known also as the axis or chital. Also within the Cervini, specifically the West

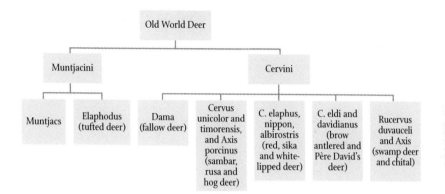

```
                          Old World Deer

        Muntjacini                              Cervini

                                        Cervus
                                      unicolor and
                                        timorensis,   C. elaphus,   C. eldi and   Rucervus
 Muntjacs    Elaphodus     Dama         and Axis       nippon,     davidianus    duvauceli
            (tufted deer) (fallow deer)  porcinus      albirostris    (brow       and Axis
                                         (sambar,     (red, sika   antlered and  (swamp deer
                                         rusa and     and white-   Père David's  and chital)
                                         hog deer)    lipped deer)    deer)
```

Figure 4 The two tribes of the Old World deer.

Eurasian Cervini, are the two fallow deer species, the European and the Persian, and, probably originating in temperate East Asia, the very large group of the red deer and wapiti, comprising four divisions. These are, first, the European, North African, Caucasian, Turkish and Northern Iranian subspecies of red deer, originating in temperate woodlands; second, the Bactrian and probably extinct Yarkand deer; third, the wapiti, including two Siberian subspecies and the North American wapiti; and fourth, a group of four Tibetan and Chinese subspecies that includes the shou.

The sika are closely related to these last two groups, as is the white-lipped or Thorold's deer, which comes from the rocky ridges of Tibet but is now well established in European zoos. Then come the Père David deer and the brow-antlered or Eld's deer. Last among the Old World deer, and separate from the large red/wapiti and sika clan above, is the important genus comprising the rusa, sambar and hog deer.[6]

We have to accept the results of genetic analysis, which often seem to contradict the visual evidence, proving apparently similar species to be unrelated. Perhaps that is why it is so

Two species of muntjac, from R. Lydekker's *The Deer of All Lands* (1898). There are 12 surviving species of muntjac, all native to South Asia. Reeves's muntjac – introduced into Britain *c.* 1925 – escaped from captivity and today is probably the most numerous species living in the wild in Britain.

19

satisfying that Sir Victor Brooke's notions based on anatomy have been so thoroughly vindicated.

Let us now look at some of the Old World deer in more detail. Among the first tribes of deer to appear was the *Muntiacini*, which later diverged into the muntjacs and the tufted deer. These two genera have almost lost their antlers in an adaptation to closed habitat, but the muntjacs compensate for their small antlers with their well-developed canine teeth, which they use for fighting other male muntjac. The tufted deer of south and central China and northeast Myanmar are significantly larger than muntjac but are closely related.

Chinese water deer, a New World deer closely related to roe, and Reeves' muntjac were both introduced to England by Herbrand Russell, the eleventh Duke of Bedford, at Woburn in about 1925. After a few years of settling in, they have thrived. Despite, or perhaps because of, their ability to reproduce all the year round, muntjac may now be England's most common deer species.

The spotted deer, chital or axis deer, from India was hitherto classed with the hog deer but sometimes it is now deemed a distant relative of it. It is twice the size of the hog deer, but the two can hybridize. Chital are very active and among the most difficult to handle in captivity of all deer, although they thrive in suitable parkland, even if they require access to shelter in temperate climates. They are, as one might expect of tropical deer, aseasonal in their breeding pattern, dropping calves in any month of the year, even when kept in parks such as that within Whipsnade zoo in England. As the popular name suggests, they retain their spots throughout their lives.

The swamp deer or barasinghas are closely related to chital, but are much more seasonal in their breeding; their natural range is in India, Pakistan and Nepal but they survive quite well

The Chinese water deer, native to China and Korea, thrives in Eastern England following its escape from captivity early in the 20th century. It has no antlers, but both sexes have long canine tusks, with which the males fight.

20

in English deer parks. A related species, Schomburgk's deer, is thought to have become extinct in the 1930s, although antlers that may have come from this species were found in a Chinese medicine shop in Laos in 1991.[7]

The European fallow is the quintessential park deer. With its distinctive palmated antlers and variously coloured coat, usually spotted, it is to urban Europeans among the most familiar of all deer. The Mesopotamian or Persian species was thought to be extinct until 1951, when relic populations were discovered in Iran; it has subsequently been introduced to Israel.

During the last interglacial the European fallow extended its range throughout much of Europe but became restricted to Anatolia after the last Ice Age. It has been transported by human agency since prehistory, perhaps more than any large mammal other than cattle, sheep and goats. There is evidence that fallow deer were moved by boat to many islands in the Mediterranean long before the domestication of cattle and sheep.[8] The Romans brought them to England but they did not become widely established until the Normans brought them from Sicily in the twelfth century.[9] Then, as a fashion accessory among landowners, they spread rapidly throughout the deer parks of Britain and Ireland.[10] They were slow to become established in mainland Europe but by the eighteenth century were widely dispersed in parks. Now fallow deer exist in the USA, Canada, the West Indies, Argentina, Chile and Peru, New Zealand and Australia, but apart from the small relic population in Turkey whence they originated, they have not colonized Asia.[11] Interestingly, fallow deer seem slow to disperse themselves when released into suitable environments and often remain within a very limited area for many decades.

The endangered Persian fallow deer are around one and a half times as large as the European fallow, and have antlers that

are much less palmated. They too were dispersed by humans
10,000 or more years ago, notably to Cyprus, where they are
now extinct.

As a result of the many genetic bottlenecks that European
fallow deer have passed through from being moved around
the world and their selection within parks, they show a variety
of coat colours based on three principal types. There is the 'common', in which the spots are barely visible in the winter but
pronounced in the summer, with a paler variation known as
'menil' in which the spots are also clearly visible in the winter;
the 'black'; and the 'white'.

Père David's deer are fond of water and have every opportunity to indulge themselves in the ponds at Woburn Abbey.

Fallow deer are thought to be the last survivor of the mega-cerines or giant deer, which included their relative, the famous but now extinct giant Irish elk.[12] This stood 2 m tall at the shoulder and carried palmated antlers weighing up to 45 kg. It only became extinct about 11,000 years ago, possibly as a result of predation by modern humans. Even this monster species was dwarfed by another megacerine of twice its weight, which was a relative of the moose.

In a separate genus within the Old World deer we find the Père David deer and the brow antlered deer or Eld's deer. The status of the beautiful Eld's deer is rather precarious. One subspecies, the Manipur, was once thought to be extinct but was rediscovered in 1951, though it still numbers less than 200. It lives on a floating mat of vegetation on the Logtak lake in Manipur, eastern India, and has feet adapted for that strange life. A second subspecies of Eld's deer, the thamin, has a wild population in Myanmar of about 1,000 and a similar number in zoos worldwide. The third subspecies of brow-antlered deer is the Thai, which is reduced to only a few dozen individuals. The Père David deer, an even larger deer, has not been known to exist outside parks within recent history and is considered extinct in the wild, although efforts are being made to re-establish it in wildlife reserves in China. Its biology and especially its propensity for water make clear that its ecological niche was wet river valleys. It is the only member of the Cervini to grow its antlers in the winter. The Père David deer is not as prolific a breeder as fallow or red deer, perhaps because of its survival from amazingly small numbers and consequent lack of genetic diversity, but nevertheless it has thrived in parks and there are large and widespread captive populations.

The Old World deer include the most spectacularly successful sub-genus, Cervus. All members form harems and carry complex antlers. This group is in a state of flux as taxonomists absorb additional data resulting from DNA studies. Until recently it was usually considered to contain three closely related sub-groups: the North American and Asian wapiti, the red deer and the sika.

The red deer may have originated more than one million years ago, probably in Asia, but did not become established until about 700,000 years ago, when together with reindeer, roe deer and moose it was first found in Europe. Populations of red deer at the western extremity of their range in Britain, Spain and Norway are among the smallest, with the largest stags rarely exceeding 230 kg. However, selection for antler trophies in a few English parks has created antlers that are more complex and heavier in relation to bodyweight than would be expected.

Red stag, from Gesner's *Historiae animalium* (1560). The male red deer was the most cherished wild animal in most of Europe for up to 50,000 years, first as the staple source of meat and later as the most revered object of the chase.

As we move east through Central Europe and western Asia, different forms of larger red deer known as maral occur, with adult stags weighing up to 350 kg in the Carpathian mountains. Within the red deer we include the only African deer, the Barbary stag of North Africa, the red deer of Corsica, four other European sub-species, and the larger maral from Caucasia, Turkey and northern Iran. Apart from its size, the maral differs from the western red deer in having a shorter tail and a larger paler rump patch, yet it is classified as the same species as its western red deer relatives. The red deer come with more cultural 'baggage' than any other deer and we will address that later, but for the time being, will merely note its enormous success in colonizing different habitats and its role as the most important quarry for humans from earliest prehistory to the present, throughout its range.

In a second small select group within the red deer clan comes the endangered Bactrian stag of Russia and Afghanistan and its probably extinct relative, the Yarkand stag from China.[13] Third come the wapiti with two Siberian sub-species, and the North American wapiti, *C.e. canadensis*, often confusingly called elk. The name wapiti is derived from the Native American Cree and Shawnee name for pale-coloured rump, and has been adopted by English-speaking people in an effort to remove the confusion caused by the use of the word 'elk'. When Europeans arrived in North America they saw large deer that they mistook for the animals with which they were familiar back home in Europe, and which they knew as 'elk'. In fact those European deer were *Alces alces*, which were also present in North America and which Americans came to call 'moose' from a word in another Native American language, Algonquian.[14] Those large American deer, which were in fact wapiti or *Cervus elaphus canadensis*, are to this day usually called elk by Americans.

The large wapiti is well equipped for northern sub-arctic conditions and has a circumpolar distribution within Asia and North America. Within America it ranges south becoming smaller so that the the Tule elk of California is the smallest, weighing up to 250 kg, while those in the Rockies in Alberta and on Vancouver Island and Alaska are the largest, and weigh more than 500 kg.

In the fourth and final of the red deer groups we find four Tibetan and Chinese sub-species: *C.e. wallichi*, known as shou, *C.e. macneilli*, *C.e. kansuensis* and *C.e. xanthopygus*. The first two of these four are either extinct or endangered, while the others

Kawanabe Ky Sai, *Landscape with Deer and Monkeys*, late 19th century, album leaf, ink and colour on silk. Despite the taunts of monkeys, these sika stags, revered in the Shinto religon, and symbolizing regeneration and longevity, remain impassive.

may exist in Chinese deer farms, probably as hybrid forms. The shou or Tibetan red deer was thought to be extinct until a group of 200 were discovered in Tibet and Bhutan in 1995; other relic populations may exist.

The white-lipped or Thorold's deer inhabits the steppes of eastern Tibet and western China as well as some Chinese deer farms and many zoos across the world. It is well adapted to cold and is about the same size as red deer with which it will hybridize. Sika – the name is taken from the Japanese word for deer – evolved earlier in Asia and spread eventually to Japan. Many sika forms evolved, but they have been so confused by millennia of deer farming and the movement of deer between parks within China that attempts to classify the different strains of sika into specific sub-species are probably doomed.[15] Inevitably genes were released into wild populations as farms were broken up in times of civil disruption. Nevertheless sika have colonized southwards into sub-tropical zones that they share with sambar, Eld's deer, hog and tufted deer and the muntjacs, and northwards, where the largest sika are found, into southeastern Mongolia and Manchuria, along with the wapiti. In addition sika inhabit much of the Japanese archipelago, where their numbers are strong and probably increasing and where their management is essentially control by culling. Conversely, in much of their Asian range sika are declining. Wapiti thrive better in cold climates than sika, extend further north and probably cope more easily with snow.

In Japan sika have long been revered and herds are still kept within temple grounds. In the nineteenth century sika were taken from China and Japan to zoos and parks in Europe and America, where again they eventually established wild populations. In Scotland sika have thrived in commercial coniferous woodland and have hybridized with red deer to such an extent that all mainland Scottish red deer populations are now, or will eventually become, genetically 'polluted'. Only on offshore islands can the Scottish red deer retain their 'purity' and there are now laws prohibiting the movement of deer onto those islands.

Along with the sika in their close relationship to the red deer and wapiti, come the rusa and sambar and the hog deer. They are tropical, almost aseasonal species inhabiting a great variety of habitats, although generally preferring thick cover; the exception is the rusa, which is a grazer. Although they are thought of as rather solitary 'hiders', they may form groups in some situations and the Javanese rusa is actually herd-forming. Rusa have been widely dispersed by humans among islands, where they are often found in smaller forms. Sambar, on the other hand, are the largest tropical deer, almost reaching the size of wapiti in the species found in the Indian sub-continent. The related hog deer, *Axis porcinus*, widespread in India and Southeast Asia, is adapted to tall and thick grassland cover, being much smaller and less gregarious.[16]

During the early Pleistocene the increase of savannah habitats meant that deer could no longer depend on hiding or slinking into dense cover to avoid predators. Instead many species of deer, like other species across the animal spectrum, adapted to open country by forming large herds: they became gregarious. Like birds that flock, or fish that shoal, this is thought to benefit the greatest number of individual animals in the group.

If one excludes the muntjacs, Old World deer are generally grazers: that is, they eat significant volumes of grass and are known as bulk feeders. Forming herds is associated with this lifestyle. They are gregarious yet non-migratory, and are well

The sika of East Asia are very common in Japan, as seen here. Their growing antlers are red and their summer coat is spotted . . .

. . . but in winter
the sika's coat
loses its spots.

adapted to resist high infestations of the tiny parasitic worms
known as nematodes that they ingest in grass that has been
soiled by other grazers. By contrast, the browser species of deer
nibble the nutritious growing tips of bushes, shrubs and herbs.
They are therefore known as concentrate selectors, and have
little ability to combat nematodes because they do not normally
eat soiled vegetation; if compelled to graze in zoos, for example,
they often succumb to parasitism. Conversely fallow and red
deer, being gregarious grazers, are well adapted to life in parks
and farms. However, in seeming contradiction to this rule,
reindeer, the only migratory deer, classed as a New World deer,
are gregarious yet especially vulnerable to parasite burdens
because their migratory lifestyle means that they are constantly
grazing clean new areas and so cannot cope with soiled pasture.
This is especially true where mild winters permit the worms to
overwinter and is perhaps the chief reason why entrepreneurs

seeking to establish herds of reindeer to pull sledges round department stores at Christmas find it more difficult than they expected. There has been a sadly high number of fatalities among the would-be Rudolphs ill-advisedly imported into England from Scandinavia over the last few years.

THE NEW WORLD DEER

All the deer tribes first appeared in central Asia but migrated into America across Beringia, now the area around the Bering Straits, at the end of the Miocene, about five million years ago. From there they radiated south, probably colonizing South America on at least two separate occasions, firstly during the early Pliocene, and later as the Pliocene gave way to the Pleistocene, about two million years ago.[17] In this they beat the Bovids, none of which ever made it to South America, and so deer were able to radiate and diversify throughout South America into different species, each exploiting a different habitat (figure 5).

Thus *Mazama*, the brocket deer, inhabits tropical forests; *Blastocerus*, the marsh deer, lives in marshes; while *Hippocamelus*, known as the huemul, and the pudu exist in the Chilean mountains; and *Ozotoceros*, the pampas deer, lives in the pampas. The pudu is the smallest of all deer; only half the size of the smallest muntjac, the northern pudu weighs only 3–6 kg. *Mazama* exists in four species and about twenty subspecies ranging in weight up to about 17 kg.

While the South American marsh deer, the pampas deer and the huemul are all endangered, among the New World deer today are also the four most populous of all deer: *Rangifer*, the caribou and reindeer; *Alces*, the moose; *Capreolus*, the roe; and *Odocoileus*, the white-tailed, black-tailed and mule deer.

Rangifer and *Alces* now exist throughout the Asian and American sub-arctic but it is thought this was a result of relatively recent dispersal into North America in the Pleistocene. Although well adapted to cold climates, roe have not become established in America.

The key species among the New World deer can be considered the white-tailed deer, *Odocoileus virginianus*, and its close relative, *O. hemionus*, the mule deer. It has colonized from north to south more effectively than any other deer in the world, and it still, in its various 38 sub-species, occupies an enormous range and diversity of habitats from southern Peru into Canada and almost to the Arctic Circle. As one might expect, its seasonal breeding is most pronounced in the north while in the equatorial regions to the south it has lost most of its seasonality.

Because of its anatomy the roe deer, *Capreolus*, is classed as a New World deer and molecular phylogeny indicates that it is closely related to *Hydropotes*, the Chinese water deer. These two are the only New World deer whose distribution is confined to the Old! In Chinese water deer the absence of antlers has been compensated for by large canine teeth, used aggressively in competition with other water deer in order to defend a food

Figure 5 The three tribes of the sub-family of 'New World Deer' or Telemetacarpalians: the Odocoileini, Capreolini and Alceini.

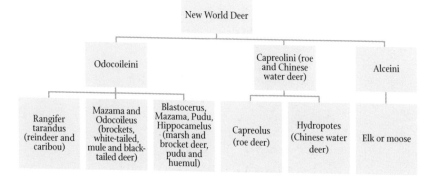

33

A roe deer from Gesner's *Historiae animalium* (1560). Fastidious eaters and highly territorial, roe deer are found throughout Europe. In North Asia they are represented by the much larger Siberian roe.

resource. Male and female bond together as a pair and each carry tusks, although the males' are much larger. Both sexes will defend their territory, which they saturate with scent from a battery of scent glands. They will also carefully place their dung to make clear to other deer that the territory is occupied and also to confuse predators.

Roe probably appeared in northern Central Europe more than 500,000 years ago but may not have reached the warmer areas of southern France, Italy and Spain for another 300,000 years. Although the Siberian roe is twice as big as the European they are both surprisingly small species to have successfully colonized cold climates. Perhaps they were assisted in this by the adaption of delayed implantation or embryonic diapause, unique to roe among deer and discussed in chapter Two. Roe deer normally bear twins and occasionally triplets; they are fastidious eaters, carefully selecting which shrubs to browse, and they are highly territorial. During the mating season the roe buck chases the doe very vigorously, stimulating her to ovulate. While European roe bucks rarely exceed 30 kg (66 lb), the Siberian roe, which live in more extreme conditions, can weigh double that.

From one of the smallest deer to the largest: the moose, or, as it is known in Europe, the elk. From a modest birth weight of 10–16 kg moose will grow to 150 kg at six months and has an adult weight of up to 600 or even 700 kg. Much lighter moose live in some less productive habitats. Moose are long-legged and this assists them in escaping from wolves, which cannot easily follow their high trotting action. Uniquely among deer, moose calves have an unspotted coat. Moose seem to have first appeared six to seven million years ago, crossing to America during the early Pleistocene. By the late Pleistocene they were found as far south as Japan and, post-Pleistocene, as far west as Ireland.

Finally, among New World deer, I must discuss the best adapted of all deer species to the arctic, *Rangifer*, the reindeer and caribou. This species seems to have evolved around five to

Sweden's Mr Moose, Sune Häggmark, has several tame moose but even so finds it advisable to cut off their antlers before the rutting season. He has adapted his Volvo car to run on dried moose dung.

Caribou bull. Caribou are the best adapted of all deer to life in the arctic, growing fast in the summer and accumulating fat reserves to help them through the winter.

six million years ago, crossing – like the moose – into North America during the early Pleistocene, around 250,000 years ago. In almost all forms of caribou and reindeer, alone among deer, both sexes grow antlers, an adaptation to permit lactating females to defend snow holes and provide feeding for their young during the arctic winter, when males and non-lactating females have cast their antlers. As one might expect, with such a gregarious and migratory lifestyle, reindeer and caribou young are precocious and able to run with their dams within a few hours of birth. They grow at an amazing speed during the short summer so as to be able to survive the winter, and produce antlers as calves.

That is a very brief résumé of the huge deer family: many with little previous experience of deer will be surprised by its diversity. Each northern temperate nation has its stereotype: Americans have taken their white-tailed deer to heart as Bambi, while Europeans, for whom the original Bambi was a roe, share Rudolph with the Americans as the reindeer with the glowing nose whom Santa Claus has enlisted to haul his Christmas sledge. In a different vein, the British have their red deer immortalized by Sir Edwin Landseer in his painting *Monarch of the Glen*. Perhaps too we can say that for most Chinese, Japanese and Asian people, deer are sika; and for Indians, chital. It is surprisingly difficult to take urban mankind beyond those stereotypes. If this chapter has served to break down the notion that all deer are the same, then I will have really achieved something.

2　How Deer Survive

When people are asked to draw deer they always sketch them with something like a hat rack on their heads: antlers. Antlers are the most conspicuous defining characteristics of the members of the deer family. And while, inevitably, the exception proves the rule – the Chinese water deer is antlerless, and the muntjac and tufted deer have only rudimentary antlers – these are secondary adaptations to life in dense cover. Their ancestors once had antlers. Thus as a general rule we can say that deer have antlers. In addition, *only* deer have antlers: no other species of any other family grows them.

As I will continue to emphasize, antlers fall off each year and regrow. Ancient observers noted this and that is why deer came to symbolize regeneration in so many cultures across the world. But the links between humans and antlers also had a practical dimension.

At Boxgrove in Surrey, England, half a million years ago – that is, several glacial periods – and long, long before Neanderthals appeared or Britain became an island, an early hominin sat with one leg stretched out and knapped a flint. There are no signs of his body, but we know this was the position he worked from because of the scatter of flint shards that fell about him. And we know that the hammer used to knap flints at Boxgrove was the base of a cast red deer antler because the archaeologists recovered that antler coronet with splinters of flint still adhering to it.[1] These early people had much smaller brains than Neanderthals or today's *Homo sapiens*, but they knew that antler was the ideal material for knapping. Thus the connection between humans and antlers extends back long before we, *H. sapiens*, arrived. The immense strength and elasticity of antler is far superior to skeletal bone and, until the development of metals, it reigned supreme not only as a material for knapping flints, but for weapon tips, sewing needles, making combs and many more tasks. There is an appealing symmetry in knowing that deer were killed with weapons tipped with flint that had been shaped using antler tools, or, even more directly, weapons tipped with antler.

Antlers are part of a survival strategy that deer have adopted in the temperate and sub-polar regions to ensure that adult males are armed for competition with other males during the intense and carefully synchronized mating season. Seasonal mating is vital to ensure that the young are born at precisely the correct time so as to draw maximum benefit from the rich spring vegetation. Although there are tropical deer with antlers, some of which are cast and regrown aseasonally, the origin of the antler as a deciduous organ lies in the northern temperate regions; the tropical deer colonized tropical regions secondarily and retained their antlers. In temperate climates and those nearer the poles, where winters are usually long and the vegetation is unproductive for many months, herbivores need to concentrate all their growth into the spring and summer so as to achieve sufficient size and energy reserves to survive the winter. Antlers are a key step in synchronizing mating to achieve that process.

Temperate climate plants are hugely productive in the long daylight hours of spring when frosts are less common. At this time, not only is growth rapid but levels of nutrition, especially protein, are dramatically higher than they are later in the summer. Of course, during the winter most plants do not grow at all. Nutritional stresses of all mammals fall most heavily on lactating females: growth of the foetus is not nearly as demanding as the production of the milk needed to feed the young. Nor, incidentally, contrary to what most men instinctively think, is the production of antlers during the summer a significant drain on the male deer's calorific input. It may temporarily deplete his mineral stores but it is nothing compared to the energy expended by the lactating female. Thus in all temperate climate herbivores, success depends on birthdates being timed so that the mothers can make best use of spring grass. It would be dangerous for all births to take place at exactly the same time because of changes in weather patterns from year to year, but the aim must be for the median calving date to be consistent from year to year. If too early, there is inadequate vegetation to sustain the mother's milk supply and the birthweight of the calf may be too low. On the other hand, a late calving risks the dam being too fat and the foetus too large, predisposing to a hazardous calving followed by a struggle to maintain good milk yield and quality as the nutritional value of the vegetation declines. Her bodyweight may then be too low to ensure conception at the optimum time that autumn and with the onset of winter, the calf may be too light to survive. Every cell in the body of temperate deer species is therefore perfectly attuned to ensure that the young are born when their mothers can draw the very best from the spring grass.[2]

Given that the gestation length is largely fixed, a synchronized calving demands a strenuous mating season with keen competition between males over a quite short period of time. This is the rut, sometimes known as the roar. During this frenzied period, male deer use every wile and strategy to attract females, bring them into heat and deter competing males.

For most people antlers are headpieces, just like the horns of the cattle, sheep, antelope and gazelles of the bovid family. But in reality, antlers are very different. The horned animals retain horns all through their lives. Horns may seem to be dead because of their hard outer layer of keratin, like our fingernails, but inside there is a bone core which is very much alive. Cutting off a horn is a significant, bloody and painful act of surgery. If an animal breaks its horn it will usually leave open a passage into a sinus, exposing it to a serious risk of infection and leaving little chance of success in future mating.

In contrast it is common for deer to break their hard antlers during fights with other males in the rutting season and although the animal may be temporarily disadvantaged for the duration

Fallow bucks with their antlers almost fully grown.

of that season, the antler is dead, so there is no pain. Unless the damage extends into the soft live tissue at the base of the antler, the new antler the next season is unaffected. The male deer can do this because their antler headpieces are, despite being bone, deciduous: dropped each year and then regrown in one of the most conspicuous marvels of nature. The regrowing antler is the fastest-growing tissue in the mammal kingdom. A big North American bull wapiti may grow his antlers at well over 2.5 cm per day, while even the smaller British red deer will achieve a daily half-inch or a modest centimetre. In addition, it is the only organ among the mammals that completely regenerates in all its complexity of skin, hairs, sweat glands, nerves, blood vessels, cartilage, bone and so on. It is not too far fetched to say that if we could only understand in depth how the growing antler differentiates all these cells, we might be some way towards enabling humans and other species to regenerate damaged spinal cord or grow new limbs.

While growing, the velvet antler is sensitive and because it is soft, it is sometimes broken. This must cause some pain, and disfigurement of the antler, but it is not normally life-threatening. The amputation of velvet antlers is illegal in Europe on welfare grounds, although in many parts of the world deer are kept on farms in order for their growing antlers to be 'harvested' for sale into the traditional Chinese medicine trade.

This wonderful and mysterious regeneration of antlers did not go unnoticed by our ancestors. Wherever people were close to deer, perhaps through hunting or through the need to collect cast antlers, the miracle of seasonal antler casting and regrowth must have been very familiar, perhaps significant but deeply mysterious. Consequently across cultures deer themselves came to symbolize regeneration, renewal and, following on from that, longevity.

Having stressed that horns are different from antlers in that they are alive, it is necessary to explain much more about the life and death of antlers. This annual cycle is divided between the 'velvet' phase, so called because the growing antler is sustained by a skin full of pulsing blood vessels covered in short hairs that resemble the plush of velvet, and the dead part of the cycle, when the antler is hard, rough and pointed.

It is never very safe to generalize across the entire deer tribe about anything, and that is certainly true in the case of antlers. Fundamentally, however, we can say that the hard, dead antlers are male sexual organs used to fight and intimidate other males of the same species while also acting as shields to protect against the thrusts of opposing males. The victor of such contests is likely to gain access to more females and disseminate his genes more widely. However this generalization immediately seems to fall down in the case of reindeer and caribou, in which species antlers are grown both by males and females. As I observed in chapter One, we can explain this away by arguing that in the harsh arctic winters, lactating females and those with calves at foot need to be armed to provide their young calves with preferential access to food, often in holes they have excavated with their feet in the snow to reach underlying plants. Mothers need antlers to defend these snow holes from other competing yearling and young adult male reindeer. Where the snow is less deep or in forests where the caribou are less densely populated and less gregarious the value of the antlers is less, and many or most females will not carry them.[3]

Another exception is the muntjac, which can mate despite having recently cast his antlers.[4] There are other exceptions, but if we take the gregarious, polygynous red deer as our example, as the mating season – the rut – approaches, male deer require hard antlers with which to challenge other males and establish their dominance. Like other features associated with the rut, including behaviour, the antlers are controlled by the male sex hormone testosterone. To watch red deer, especially those living in open country rather than wooded cover, engaging in the rut is to witness one of the great spectacles of wildlife. Through August and September, under the influence of high testosterone levels, the stag has doubled the girth of his neck so that he could easily turn a car over. His neck mane has become long and shaggy, and his testicles have so enlarged that the white scrotum bulges conspicuously between his hind legs. He ceases grazing during the period of the rut so as to better chivvy his hinds to test whether they are on heat and will stand for him to mate them. He roars incessantly, thrashes the ground, wallows, waves his penis about and creates the maximum noise and smell. The effect of this is to stimulate the females to ovulate and increase his chances of procreation, preferably during October. At the same time the serious business of seeing off challengers is going on. If an interloper is not intimidated by the incumbent stag's big antlers and body and his vigorous roaring and other activity, he may enter into a 'parallel walk', each stag walking slowly and deliberately, separated by a few metres, in a tense march interrupted by bouts of antler thrashing and roaring. One of the stags may run for it, seeing discretion as the better part of valour, or the contest may culminate in a fight. This may be a mere clash or, more rarely, it may last for half an hour or more.

During all this activity stags lose up to one-fifth of their body weight, and their livers turn yellow, like those of a starved human. In addition, rutting stags produce a pungent odour in their urine, which they spray on themselves and their surroundings. It is also during this time that the antlers are tested, frequently to breaking point. Whole antlers may break off and

The head of a red stag that has just cast his right antler, from which blood is still flowing; a new left antler, replacing one cast a day or two earlier, is already growing.

even, occasionally, in mineral-deficient areas where antlers may be less strong, a stag can lose both antlers. More frequently only one or two points are broken. Since they are made of dead tissue, the stag feels no pain from the fracture. Unlike the horned animal, those antler breakages can be made good during the next antler growth period, in the months of sexual quiescence. During the 1960s and 1970s a group of scientists from Cambridge University studied the red deer on the Isle of Rum off the west of Scotland; it was noted that a stag named Cecil used to regularly break off both antlers during fights and pass the winter without any. The next year there he was again at the rutting grounds, armed with a new set.

In areas where the ground is depleted of minerals deer will sometimes gnaw cast antlers; in fact, I have even seen them gnaw their colleagues' antlers before they are cast! This gnawing is not seen in places where mineral levels are normal.

So much for the endpoint, the hard, dead, weapon. What has happened to the stag to let him reach this point in the annual cycle? To continue using our red deer model a little longer, we can say that the hard antler, perhaps in the absence of a few points broken off in the heat of the rut, will be carried through the long winter against a background of declining levels of testosterone in his blood. The antlers may be used playfully in spars with other stags and to enforce dominance but their main role is over. After the rut the blood levels of testosterone fall and continue a gradual depletion as the testicles reduce production of this hormone and dwindle in size. They reach baseline levels by early spring. It is then that the cells known as osteoclasts, whose role it is to digest bone, gather at the base of the antler below the coronet and do their work so rapidly that a stag may one day be playfully, but nevertheless forcefully, rattling his antlers with another stag and the next day those very antlers will fall off. Generally one antler will fall within about 24 hours of the other. The stag carries his head for a few moments in such a way as to suggest that the process of antler casting is painful and there is normally a trickle of blood. However the blood of red deer congeals quickly and the bright red raw surface soon becomes a dark purple clot and then a healing wound. At the same time as those osteoclasts were congregating the new antler was beginning to grow, so that by the time the old antler is cast the new antler is clearly visible as a black velvet ring around the casting surface.

The 'velvet' antler, which grows under the wound, soon begins to swell upwards, carrying the vestiges of the scab with it. During the early summer the antler grows rapidly, as we have seen; a

very large red deer stag may grow antlers weighing 10 or 15 kg before growth slows as the summer solstice is passed.

In the white-tailed deer, mule deer, reindeer, caribou and moose the antlers are cast gradually during the autumn and winter and the new antler will not start to grow till the spring, while in the roe the antlers are grown during the winter. But for most temperate deer species the antlers grow during the summer. We can picture red deer stags or fallow bucks lying lazily in a tight group in the shade of an ancient tree on a hot summer's day. They ruminate or cud, flicking their ears incessantly against the flies, with their eyes half-closed but always with their heads surmounted by increasingly impressive growing velvet antlers. It is these amazing regenerating organs that have so grasped the minds of a large proportion of the world's population. For, from central Russia eastwards, throughout China and Korea and south into Vietnam and Thailand, and worldwide within the Chinese diaspora in North America and Europe, Southeast Asia and Australasia, the whole of a deer is a valued part of the traditional Chinese pharmacopeia associated with longevity and renewal. Though all parts of the deer are thought to be imbued with health-giving properties, especially the penis, the foetus, the sinews of the legs, the tail and the heart, the growing antler is valued above all else.[5] These tissues are all seized upon and believed to be panaceas but there is a general belief in traditional Chinese medicine that male potency is an element of good health and that velvet antler is especially effective in restoring it. This is something of a paradox given that at the time of antler growth, when the antlers are clothed in velvet, testosterone, the male sex hormone, is at its nadir with circulating levels almost undetectably low. It is strange that velvet antler is so highly valued for its aphrodisiac qualities when in fact it is so singularly lacking in testosterone. Nevertheless some scientists believe that,

The head of a stag six weeks after antler casting with the crown points just differentiating. Having grown at perhaps one or two centimetres per day, now growth is beginning to slow as the longest day has passed.

Antler and other deer products for sale outside a medicine shop in Seoul, South Korea. These hard antlers have probably come from Asian wapiti in eastern Russia.

reflecting its uniquely rapid growth, the velvet antler contains compounds that may be beneficial in, for example, speeding up wound healing in humans.

In response to declining day length at the summer solstice, the pineal gland increases production of melatonin, which leads by a complex chemical chain to a gradual increase in the levels of circulating testosterone. The antler – which as it grew had a strength and consistency comparable to, say, a carrot – now begins to harden. The growing antler is made up largely of cartilage, the tissue that normally precedes bone. Minerals are deposited in this cartilage and by the middle of August the 'velvet' skin is beginning to break up and die. Flies are attracted to it and the velvet hangs down as strips for a few days until the stag cleans it off by thrashing his new white antlers on trees and bushes. Very soon the freshly dead antler is burnished brown with only the tips polished white. This is the culmination of the entire cycle; the objective has been achieved and the dangerous antlers, hugely strong and hard, are ready to do their work. Testosterone levels are high again and the stag migrates to his rutting grounds once more.

The body of the hard antler is rough and fissured with the route of the blood vessels that travelled through the velvet still visible as furrows. This roughness, known as pearling, is valued by trophy collectors. The stag can immediately use his new antlers for thrashing and for sparring with other stags, which perhaps allows him to develop a feel for the shape and space they occupy. They will see him through the mating season or rut as vital weapons of offence and defence, allowing him to defeat other stags and gain access to females.

In 1986 George Darwall and Rob Clark published a fascinating and very simple mathematical hypothesis as to how antlers might develop their strange shapes.[6] Using only two-dimensional

The antlers are fully grown, hardened, and this fallow buck is cleaning his velvet ready for the autumn rut.

The hard antler on a rutting stag is a formidable weapon, and when stags have lost their fear of humans they are very dangerous. This stag is roaring and making his intention to charge very clear.

modelling within the limits of the computers of the day, they suggested that a variable number of growth points might exist on the surface of the pedicle, the living bony outgrowth of the skull that is exposed when the old antler is cast. They proposed that these growth points comprise rapidly dividing cells that spread over the surface and then move steadily up the growing antler. We now know that it is indeed stem cells within the membrane, the periosteum, overlying the pedicle, that play a crucial role in antler growth.[7] We also know that the front part of the pedicle periosteum is the most likely to control growth of the brow point, and that the central part is the most active in antler regeneration.

If each growing point is assumed to exercise an inhibiting effect on neighbouring growth points, the results are complex antler-like shapes. Thus computer models hypothesizing the existence of three points will create a shape that resembles a roe buck's antler, while five points comes closer to that of the fallow deer. Stags with multipoint antlers can be assumed to have developed additional growth points further up the antler, which cause branching and create higher degrees of complexity.

One of the most bizarre features of antler growth is the effect of injury. This is most often observed in deer that have fractured a leg. Such animals usually show a remarkable capacity for survival and will often make good the fracture and 'go sound' again. Occasionally this is even seen in deer that have a compound fracture in which the fractured bone is protruding through the skin. If the deer are growing antlers when the injury takes place they will manifest an asymmetry of antler growth that seems almost inexplicable. In 1972 American workers published the results of an experiment, which I hope would now be considered unethical, in which they had amputated hind limbs from three white-tailed bucks and confirmed that the contralateral antlers all grew deformed for the next two years.[8] Injuries may be 'remembered' by growing antlers for up to ten years.

I know from repeated personal observation that the effect is also present even if the injury does not result in a fracture. It seems that the stimulus is most probably longstanding pain. These observations are even more enigmatic when one considers that cutting the nervous supply to the antlers does not by itself affect antler growth, as was demonstrated by two scientists, George B. Wislocki and Marcus Singer, in 1946.[9]

It has been suggested that the response of the growing antler to chronic pain may be mediated through a release of endorphins, 'the body's own morphine', but how that affects the antler is not clear. Neither is it understood how it can specifically influence the contralateral antler. It is hard to escape the conclusion that some neural pathway must be involved.

Generally deer species become larger and carry bigger, more complex antlers as they extend into temperate regions, but there are very clear exceptions to this: the Chinese water deer and some muntjac species are small temperate-climate animals, while the large sambar are certainly tropical, yet may reach 200 kg, although they retain simple three-pronged antlers. The smaller tropical deer are almost all of a height comparable with a Labrador dog, although they only weigh around 10–20 kg. These small deer depend on having adequate food resources throughout the year, so they do not need to store fat for lean times. They achieve this by living in woodland or, in the case of Chinese water deer, wet floodplains. Usually in temperate climates deer need to capitalize on seasonal abundance in the spring and summer to allow them to accumulate reserves that will carry them through the winter. To do this they need to be large. Roe deer, another obvious exception, inhabit temperate woodland where there are few competitors and sufficient food. Even so, the Siberian roe deer living further north needs to be much larger than its temperate-climate relative, the European roe.

The European roe, ranging from southern Europe to the Arctic, is only about 25 kg in weight. This is only about one-eighth the weight of red deer, with which they geographically overlap. In the east of Asia the European roe gives way to the Siberian, which is approximately twice the size of the European. For deer the size of European roe, we would expect a gestation length of perhaps five months. However, given the necessity of giving birth in the spring, this would demand a rut in the middle of winter. That would be energetically very costly in their cold temperate range and the roe has avoided that by delaying the implantation of the fertilized egg into the wall of the womb. Thus, although roe rut and mate in July and August, the fertilized

An assymmetric antler on a stag that had sustained an injury. How does the injury influence the growing antler? This remains a mystery but is undoubtedly a fact.

egg remains loose within the womb as a minute embryo until December, when it implants and begins an effective five-month gestation to permit a spring birth, usually of twins. This permits the buck to enjoy a vigorous rut during the summer, when he eagerly chases the does, often in small circles, for many minutes, which is probably necessary to induce them to ovulate. It had been thought that it was the change in day length associated with the winter solstice that stimulated the seemingly inert embryo into growth, but it seems clear from several studies that the duration of embryonic inactivity is fixed and that it is actually the summer solstice that stimulates the doe to come into heat, within only about one month of the longest day. Thereafter the length of pregnancy is about 293 days. Of this artificially long gestation, development only occurs from around the winter solstice to birth, about five months.[10]

This cunning scheme has certainly proved effective for roe deer, which have been among the most successful deer species over the last 50 years. They are rapidly increasing in numbers throughout Europe. In Britain they have risen from near-extinction in the nineteenth century to populate the entire mainland, including many suburban sites, in the same way as has the white-tailed deer in North America. Roe and white-tailed deer occupy very similar niches and it is their ability to adapt to diverse environments under reduced hunting pressures, as the human population becomes increasingly urbanized, that must explain their success.

Although deer are sophisticated herbivores that normally survive by eating a wholly vegetable diet, many will eat small mammals and birds if they get the chance. Muntjac, for example, will seek out and eat eggs, young birds and small mammals. Incidentally muntjac are also probably largely responsible for almost eliminating the nightingale from England, not by eating them but by destroying the bushy undergrowth in oak woodland. Red deer on the Isle of Rum off the west of Scotland have famously been described as killing and eating Manx shearwaters. They do this by trampling them with their forefeet and then biting their heads off as the seabirds return at night to their burrows on the tops of mountains to feed their young. The red deer on my farm sometimes kill weak or diseased rabbits by pounding them with their forefeet, and will then eat them. They even compete with each other if I throw them a freshly killed rabbit, and the victorious hind will then carefully eat the head and limbs, leaving just a neat torso. I have seen them spend an hour doing that. White-tailed deer have been precisely recorded as eating up to nine dead fish (alewives) per minute when these were washed ashore, as well as dead birds and beetles. Reindeer, inhabiting perhaps the most demanding terrain of all deer, are enthusiastic eaters of meat. Like white-tailed deer they will eat dead fish washed up on a shore line, but they will also hunt live lemmings and eat dead ones, and gnaw bones. Reindeer will also seek out the urine of humans or dogs and lick sweat from human limbs.[11] Nevertheless, having said all that, deer have obviously evolved to eat vegetation – they are clearly not well adapted to a hunting lifestyle. They have mobile muzzles and upper lips that allow them to select particular plants and grasses. Deer, like many other ruminant species such as sheep and cattle, have lost their upper incisor teeth and instead carry a hard pad against which the lower incisors can grip so that the vegetation is pulled out. This allows the softest and most nutritious parts of the stems of grass or plants to be taken in.

The great success of many species of deer lies in their ability to digest quantities of low-grade vegetation and process it quickly through their stomachs and intestines. With this aptitude they were able to colonize the growing grasslands of the drier, cooler early Pleistocene and establish themselves in cool temperate climates by making the all-important adaptations to seasonality that characterize most modern deer species.

The way in which any herbivore eats and digests is fundamental to its lifestyle. As we have seen, deer are ruminants. They have a complex stomach made up of four chambers, sometimes described as four stomachs. Animals which eat that most indigestible but often plentiful substrate, grass, are adapted to filling their largest stomach, the rumen, with as much as they can forage as quickly as possible. Then they lie up, often in a large group to provide protection from predators. They don't sleep but ruminate, and the electrical pattern in the brain of ruminating herbivores resembles that of sleeping single-stomach species. If you watch a ruminant, such as a cow, ruminating you can see wads of vegetation moving up the neck and into the mouth, where they can be thoroughly masticated between the ridged cheek teeth before being visibly consigned back down into the rumen. In other words, as they lie up and rest, these animals regurgitate the rumen contents and break up the strong fibres and cellulose-walled cells of the grass with their teeth, then return the wad of grass to the rumen for fermentation by abundant bacterial flora. In cattle the rumen is enormous, perhaps holding as much as 225 litres. For obvious reasons these grass-devouring animals have been called 'bulk feeders'. Among deer the closest we come to bulk feeders are members of the Old World species: the red/wapiti/sika group and fallow deer, as well as, for example, the Père David, are well adapted to thrive on grassland parks and farms. Associated with this strategy, they are highly gregarious and tend to form harems during the rut. Given that polygamous life style, the male is much larger than the female and they have evolved complex antlers. Normally the females will only bear one young.

In contrast, the smaller 'concentrate selectors' inhabit a more diverse habitat and carefully select the protein-rich growing tips of a large variety of different plants. For these species the ability to ruminate is less important. Indeed, in the simpler concentrate selector species, such as muntjacs, the rumen is only partially developed, carrying two blind chambers. Perversely, Chinese water deer, which are certainly not gregarious, are classed as intermediate in that they are well adapted to eating richly varied vegetation beside rivers that regularly flood. The most obviously concentrate selecting deer are almost solitary, living in small family groups. The females are almost as large as the males; they tend to produce several young; antlers are usually very basic; and these deer can be described as hiders, normally inhabiting thick cover within which they are territorial.

Although the theory of bulk feeder, concentrate selector and intermediate ruminant digestion has had to be developed and refined since it was first proposed by R. R. Hofmann in the 1980s, it nevertheless provides an important way of comparing and contrasting the vast array of strategies and anatomical variations that have been brought to bear on the problem of digesting vegetation.[12] The enormous variation within the family of deer spans that spectrum and each species has created its own niche to accommodate almost infinitely diverse combinations of climate, vegetation, competitors and predators.

3 The Exploitation of Deer

Wild animals are the flip side of the downtrodden brute domestic animal: they are mysterious, ethereal, evanescent, here one minute and gone the next, melting into the shadows, 'will-o'-the-wisp'. We watch wild animals and envy their independence. We invest them with superstition. They are noble and proud. Compare these free spirits with the domestic animal: the beast of burden, obedient and subservient, the antithesis of its wild forgotten ancestors, an object of pity.

Proximity and familiarity breed contempt and early man came close to deer, so perhaps for them deer were not thought quite so wild. Yet, even if tamed, few species of deer have ever been domesticated. The question of why is a puzzle that has never been solved. It is of interest because the domestication of crops and livestock was perhaps humanity's greatest step, slowly opening the door to a static lifestyle, writing, possessions, cities and empires. Deer, with the single exception of reindeer, played little or no part in this. Mankind had abundant opportunity to domesticate the deer, especially elk and red and fallow deer in Europe, but that step was never taken until modern times, when red deer finally came to be domesticated on New Zealand farms.[1]

From deep in prehistory, many peoples have captured and handled deer. The evidence for this lies, for example, in their

dispersal to islands. Mesopotamian fallow deer were translocated to Cyprus 9,000 or 10,000 years ago and European fallow to Rhodes and other Mediterranean islands about 1,000 years later. The Scottish Outer Hebrides were stocked with red deer by at least the Bronze Age and Orkney during the Neolithic. Other translocations of rusa and axis deer took place among the islands of Southeast Asia and the Pacific.[2]

That early people so long ago had the organization and skills to capture live deer, restrain them in small boats and convey them to offshore islands is remarkable. How did they do it? Early hunting systems entailed driving deer either through narrow defiles or into enclosures. It is not unreasonable to suppose that young calves might be captured in this way, and

Stags in the half-light of a misty morning. The image of deer as ephemeral wild animals briefly glimpsed contributes to their mystery and allure, fuelling their symbolic role.

perhaps even kept alive with the limited resources of available food. There are historical accounts of deer being breastfed by Maya women and in some societies today, such as the endangered nomadic Amazonian tribe the Awa-Guajá, and in India the Bishnoi, wild animals are still occasionally breastfed by women. Red deer were hand-reared and trained as decoys to assist hunters by the Romans, whose mosaics illustrate them being led on leads. And there are historical records of tame decoy deer being used in many civilizations, including in China. Such decoys must have been more effective than the stalking horses, which appear in some medieval illustrations and can surely never have fooled the deer.

What remains a mystery is why such intimate and ancient contact with deer never led to more general domestication. Until the recent development of deer farming in New Zealand, only the reindeer herders of northern Asia could be said to have actually domesticated deer. To colonize the most hostile environments on Earth, humanity has had to ride on the back – often literally – of the animal species that have evolved to survive in those climates. Thus, just as hot, arid deserts have become accessible to humanity through exploitation of the camel, reindeer have provided the key to man's survival in the arctic. In the very hostile environment from northern Fenno-Scandinavia east across Northern Asia, since the retreat of the glaciers and the first humans reaching the region, there have been many tribes that have exploited reindeer in different ways. Some merely follow the migrations of the deer, mustering and killing them, but others variously use them for milk production, for riding or for haulage. In every case, as with hunting peoples, the reindeer provides its meat for food; its hides for many uses, including clothing; its sinews for sewing and for lashing snowshoes and sledges; its hair for insulation and decoration;

its bones for tools and wind instruments; and its antlers for weapons and implements. Yet the reindeer of these northern Asian people, although almost identical in appearance, are temperamentally very different from the undomesticated caribou of North America. Reindeer are undeniably domesticated, yet caribou are wild, and the Inuit peoples of the high Arctic in America remain resolutely hunters, while for the most part their Asian counterparts became reindeer herders.

For the Canadian government, armed with paternal zeal during the 1920s, it seemed that the caribou's reluctance to be tamed was the principal reason why the Inuit remained hunters

This reindeer herder's clothing is stitched from reindeer skins, his sledge is laden with pelts; even his tent is covered with hides.

rather than herders. That may be so, but perhaps there is also something in the Inuit temperament that is incompatible with pastoralism. Nevertheless a scheme was developed whereby a significant number of reindeer would be herded across the Alaskan peninsular into the Mackenzie River basin within the Canadian Northwest Territories to create a reindeer reserve. This was intended to allow the Inuit there to establish the skill of reindeer herding and avoid the periodic famines that seemed inseparable from a life of caribou hunting. When the journey started in 1929, it was anticipated that the trek of 1,800 miles would be achieved in only eighteen months, but it was not to be: starting with 3,000 reindeer, the mixed team of Saami and Inuit herders experienced births, marriages and deaths along the road, finally delivering 2,370 animals five years later.

Domestication entails genuine genetic change into a more tractable and docile animal; it is very different from taming. There are many instances of deer being tamed. The Swedish king Charles XI established a courier service based on moose-drawn sleighs, which were fast and reliable, but his attempt to establish a moose-mounted cavalry failed. In Siberia moose were often ridden, but when Ivan the Terrible sent the Cossack Timofeyevich to conquer Siberia in the sixteenth century he prohibited the taming of moose, because they could easily out-run the Cossacks on horseback. Moose travel fast by trotting and could outrun horses when pulling sleighs. In addition, moose cause horses to panic, and it was for this reason that they were banned from the streets of Tartu in Estonia in the eighteenth century.[3]

Elector Frederick III of Brandenberg, later Frederick I of Prussia, is reported to have killed a famous red deer stag bearing 66 points on its antlers at Moritzburg near Dresden in 1696, but only because the gamekeeper's daughter riding a tame moose was able to drive the stag within range. So highly valued was this outstanding trophy that it was subsequently exchanged by Frederick I's successor with Frederick Augustus of Saxony for a company of the tallest grenadiers to be found in Saxony, intended as the king of Prussia's bodyguard.[4] Already antler trophies were prized very highly in Germany.

Cow moose can be milked. They browse in the forest and then learn to enter the milking shed punctually. Milking extends the normal lactation period, and increases production from the natural 75–100 litres up to 150 litres. One recorded case totalled 429 litres.[5] An Egypto-Roman plaster cast dated to 200 BC shows a moose being milked.[6]

All descriptions of moose domestication indicate that it depends on bottle-raising calves, which must be taken within less than three days of birth so as to imprint on the surrogate mother. They will then become extremely tractable and deeply associated with their fosterer. Experiments in Russia conducted from the 1950s explored their ability as milk producers, as draught animals and for meat. The calmest bulls were castrated for draught purposes, because intact bull moose are unmanageable during the rut. Both sexes are really only able to be worked for about 60 per cent of the year.

Moose need natural browse to remain healthy and, as mentioned before, they are very susceptible to malignant catarrhal fever, which is carried by healthy sheep. It is probably for these reasons that they have never been routinely domesticated for protracted historical periods.

Sune Häggmark, known as Mr Moose in Sweden, has a number of tame moose and uses the dung from them to fuel his Volvo car, which has a heat exchanger in the boot which he claims will get him from his home the 550 km to Stockholm with only three refills. He has also processed the dung into paper on which he prints banknotes for his tourist visitors.

Red deer have been tamed on several occasions, usually by eccentric aristocrats. One of these was George Walpole, third Earl of Orford, who in about 1750 regularly harnessed four red deer stags to his phaeton. The local staghounds once took chase and hunted him from Bury Hill outside Newmarket into the inn yard at the Rutland Arms, where the stags were normally stabled. Luckily a groom closed the gates against the hounds and saved the day. It is not always easy to distinguish fact from legend: it is reputed that an eccentric named Margat mounted his pet stag, Coco, and had the pair of them hoisted by a hot air balloon in 1817. St Kentigern (alias Mungo), the first bishop of Glasgow, is supposed to have harnessed a stag to his plough. Reputedly Abbot Thokey had the body of Edward II carried to 'the Abbey' from Gloucester 'in his own chariot drawn by stags'.[7]

In the nineteenth century, Americans in the west, confronted with new species of deer and with the pioneer spirit still alight, often used their skills in breaking horses and handling cattle to train moose and wapiti. Courtland Du Rand, for example, drove around his ranch in Montana drawn by a pair of wapiti, and had four others he used as pack animals.[8]

The Père David deer have never been known outside parks, yet they remain undomesticated. Discovered in 1865 by the French Jesuit Père David in the imperial hunting park near Peking, some animals were successfully transported back to Europe, where a very few individuals were introduced to Woburn by Herbrand Russell, the eleventh Duke of Bedford, between 1893 and 1895. All other populations, including those in China, became extinct by about 1920, but fortunately they have flourished at Woburn and some animals have been returned to China. This species probably became extinct in the wild

2,000 or 3,000 years ago, and yet despite their long period of living in parks, they remain wild and untamed.

The same is true of the several species of deer retained in captivity in Asian countries in order to have their growing antlers amputated each year to produce velvet antler for the traditional Chinese medicine trade. Until recently, few of these deer were being selectively bred for docility, although no doubt selection for antler size was practised centuries ago. Now, for sika, this has become an organized and technically sophisticated exercise in animal breeding. Sambar, rusa, hog deer, white-lipped deer and Siberian wapiti are all involved in the industry in one place or another. The effectively wild animals are usually kept in concrete pens in intensive farming conditions. It seems inevitable that these deer will become domesticated. Artificial insemination and even embryo transfer are increasingly used to hybridize the farmed deer species so as to maximize velvet antler production in China, trophies in America, New Zealand and Europe, and venison in New Zealand.

Many have commented that the one million red deer now being farmed in New Zealand are merely tamed, yet by all definitions we they can state categorically that these animals are domesticated, and can lay claim to be the first new livestock species in at least 5,000 years. They have passed through many generations on farms; they are selectively bred, regularly handled and treated against disease; the calves are weaned, the stags' antlers are removed annually, and ultimately they are killed in abattoirs.

And what about the fallow deer? With only a relic population left in its natural range in Anatolia, this species has been translocated to many parts of the Old and New Worlds by human agency. Their introduction into Britain by the Romans was not, it is believed, successful in establishing a resident population.

PÈRE DAVID'S DEER.

Nor does it seem as though fallow deer became widespread in mainland Europe until perhaps the sixteenth century.[9] Even where wild populations have been established, they disperse only very slowly: five centuries after the first fallow deer were placed on Inchmurrin, an island on Loch Lomond, Scotland, they have not dispersed much further than the lochside. Nor in New Zealand have fallow spread far from their original site of introduction compared to other species. Yet fallow deer are capable of becoming very tame, and it has been been suggested that their Latin name, *Dama dama*, shares the same stem as domestic, dame and even tame, although it is normally thought of as deriving from the Latin word for pale coloured.[10] Yet despite these close connections with mankind, including their existence in deer parks for many centuries, they cannot be described as ever having been domesticated.[11]

At the time of the Norman Conquest in 1066, there seem to have been no fallow deer in England, but the invaders soon changed all that by introducing them, almost certainly from

Père David deer, from R. Lydekekker, *Deer of All Lands* (1898). At the time of its publication the entire population was reduced to less than 20.

These sika, penned on concrete on a Chinese deer farm, are typical of thousands kept to provide their growing antlers each year for the traditional Chinese medicine trade.

Less frequently, as here in Inner Mongolia, sika are herded on grass.

This European fallow buck with his characteristic palmated antlers and tassled prepuce is ready for the rut with massively developed neck muscles.

Sicily, which they had recently conquered. The Domesday Book of 1086 mentions only 37 parks but well over 100 *haiae*, sometimes in connection with deer.[12] The parks were deer parks, but we don't know exactly what *haiae* were. Probably they were places into which deer, perhaps most often roe deer, were driven and captured or killed, but they may also have been places in which deer were enclosed, as in parks. It seems likely that *haiae* were Saxon in origin while parks were perhaps Norman. In any case, it is clear that some sort of enclosures for handling or keeping deer were well established by the time the Normans arrived. Many more followed. It has been estimated that over 3,000 deer parks were founded in England and Wales over the next 200 years and almost all of these seem to have been stocked with fallow deer. This represents perhaps the largest confinement of wild animals in recorded history anywhere in the world. Some of these were the indigenous red deer, but

most were fallow. Roe deer are extremely difficult to maintain in a park, although they can quite easily be driven into nets or other catching systems.

Fallow deer had all the prerequisites for becoming fashion accessories. They were novel; they were beautiful, with their spotted coats, and perhaps even then they had different colours; they had big antlers – in fact fallow deer have bigger antlers in relation to their body weight than any other deer – and above all, they were associated with the victorious Norman conquerors, the new upper class. The fashion for deer parks was set. They were hunted within the park either by coursing or by 'bow and stable', or occasionally *'par force des chiens'* (with hounds). The associated complexities of managing the deer included winter feeding, occasional live capture for stocking other parks, deterring park breakers and maintaining the park pales, normally a ditch and a mound surmounted by either a live, 'quick', hedge or a dead paling, usually of cleft oak palings or, especially later, walls of stone or brick.[13]

The history of Britain's deer parks is long and fascinating. Always constructed to aggrandize their owners, they graduated from providing hunting and venison to becoming advertisements of conspicuous waste. Thus in the sixteenth century, deer parks became accessories to the big new houses of the Tudor grandees. In 1519 François I of France commenced the building of his extraordinary hunting lodge at Chambord, with its park of 13,600 acres surrounded by a 20-mile wall. He is reputed to have progressed there with 12,000 horsemen. It is this example that is thought to have inspired Henry VIII to develop Hampton Court and Nonsuch Palaces, with their huge parks. When Elizabeth I came to the throne, she inherited 200 parks. While Britain was not alone in having deer parks, it seems to have had many more than other European countries.

Franco-Flemish tapestry of a stylized deer park, c. 1500. The park improbably contains fruit trees despite the presence of both red and fallow deer, and the Fountain of Life. The robust palings and locked door reveal affinities with paradise and the *hortus conclusus*.

The parks changed subtly from being openly ostentatious places in which monarchs and nobles could be seen hunting, to more private enclosures behind walls, which impressed by their uselessness and by the venison that could be gifted to create an impression. Extraordinary crenellated deer houses in which the animals could be fed, such as those at Sudbury and Bishop Auckland, were built during the eighteenth and nineteenth centuries. Deer were coursed for bets in the parks along carefully constructed tracks in front of grandstands, and later so that they could be captured, castrated and stall-fed. This prevented them from rutting, when they lose so much weight, and thus provided a secure source of fat venison for Christmas. The royal family housed and fed castrated deer in stalls at Windsor until 1921.[14]

Ultimately the parks became carefully designed landscapes in which deer were intended to convey an aura of the wild and untamed, yet were clearly controlled by the landowner. Much

The deer cote at Sudbury, Derbyshire, built in 1723, is typical of deer houses constructed in English deer parks. They were used to store hay, for feeding, and were perhaps also places for shooting deer.

This 18th-century drawing shows how red deer were coursed by hounds into a net so they could be captured and transported to other parks. The scene is Richmond Park near London.

more prosaically, the grazing of deer created a perfect sward free of unsightly sheeptracks or cowpats.

Many ecologists and anthropologists now think that parkland landscape is the closest to the wild woodland savanna that man has inhabited for tens of thousands of years in the north temperate Holocene, and that it is the landscape to which we are psychologically best adapted. Maybe that is why we enjoy golf courses, as well as the remaining deer parks.

Given the very close connection between people and their most popular quarry, the red deer, in Western Eurasia from the Mesolithic onwards, this species is perhaps the most likely candidate for domestication. Not only was it the principal object of the hunt, and the staple meat in much of Eurasia, but its antler was a great prize. For many people in Holocene, post-glacial Europe and Asia, the chief value of deer lay in its antlers. As a tool in its own right or for knapping flints into useful shapes, the antler of red deer was of inestimable value. Contemporary with the construction of Stonehenge, flint was being mined on an industrial scale at several sites in England. The Neolithic flint mines at Grimes Graves in East Anglia comprise some 500 mine shafts, each of which is thought to have consumed at least 150 antlers. These were used as picks by the miners between 4,000 and 5,000 years ago. You can still descend one of these shafts to experience a little of what it must have been like down there in the dark, hacking out lumps of flint. The miners used red deer antlers for their work because they make ideal picks. Other Neolithic uses for antler include the construction of long

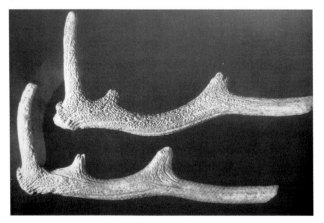

Antler picks from Grime's Graves, Norfolk, that were used to mine the flints at about the same time as Stonehenge was being developed over 4,000 years ago. Tens of thousands of antlers were used at these mines and many still retain the handprints of their users in the clay that coats them.

75

barrows, mounds such as at Silbury Hill, the largest artificial prehistoric mound in Europe, causewayed enclosures, and henges such as Stonehenge itself. The demand for antler must have been huge. Some archaeologists have pondered how so many antlers could have been gathered; they fall off in the spring and are rapidly overgrown with vegetation, so unless the grass is very short and there is little other growth, finding antlers is difficult, as many deer keepers will testify.

For years I pondered why red deer were not domesticated and how our forbears managed to find so much antler. Then I read the diary of Celia Fiennes, describing her visit to the New Forest in the late seventeenth century. In her inimitable way, she describes watching the keepers manage their deer by feeding them browse:

> at these severall Lodges the Keepers gather Brouce and and at certaine tymes in the day by a call gathers all the Dear in within the railes which belongs to each Lodge and so they come up and feed upon this Brouce and are by that meanes very fatt and very tame so as to come quite to eate out of your hand; all the day besides they range about and if they meete any body, if it be their own keeper, without the pail of the Lodge will run from him as wild as can be; these Lodges are about four miles asunder and it's a great priviledge and advantage to be a Cheefe Keeper of any of these Lodges, they have venison as much as they please and can easily shoote it when the troop comes up with in the paile.[15]

What Fiennes described was probably so commonplace that it went largely unrecorded. It was certainly not unique. In North America the Chippewa people, for example, used to cut white

cedar trees so as to attract deer which they could then shoot. Experience with wild deer in Scotland on the Isle of Rum and at many Highland estates has made it clear how simple it is to train deer to come and feed. Sound a vehicle horn, and deer will run more than a mile for a handful of maize. Such a simple expedient must have been equally available to prehistoric people. Could it be that those Mesolithic folk understood that by collecting browse which the deer could not reach and feeding it to the animals they could retain them in a small area at the time of antler casting? We know from the behaviour of deer today that it would have been eminently feasible. Red deer cast their antlers in early spring, March, when they are at their hungriest. The provision of forage would have been especially welcome to the stags and they are then most easily attracted to feed. In addition, at that time their aggression is at its nadir, so they do not fight. Perhaps the deer were even confined by the

Wild red deer attracted to hay at Glen Muick, Scotland. Our ancestors used fodder such as ivy to attract wild deer into easy bow range. This must also have made collecting cast antlers much easier.

use of natural and man-made hedges in clearings in woodland during the few weeks around the time of antler casting. Given the savanna or parkland structure of woodland in the Neolithic, it might not have been beyond the capability of people to have actually constructed ditches or hedges to have enclosed deer, at least during the period of antler casting. It would then have been easy to pick up the cast antlers.[16]

Very high counts of ivy pollen have been reported from some Mesolithic settlement sites, and it has been suggested that ivy was gathered for feeding to deer. Ivy is very popular with red deer, and it is easily gathered by people, even when it has been browsed as high as the deer can reach. Ivy would be the ideal browse to draw deer to feed.

Although antlers are dropped each spring and regrow through the summer, larger antlers are only produced by older stags. Consequently, if a herd of red deer is to provide significant quantities of large antlers, it will need to include a disproportionate number of adult stags. Adult male red deer cannot easily be handled and, once they are tame and have lost their fear of humans, red deer stags and even fallow and roe bucks are desperately dangerous and will try to kill anyone who comes near them. This has been one of the main reasons given for the fact that red deer have not been domesticated. Yet if deer are free-ranging and only tempted in to feed in the spring, when they are hungriest and their levels of aggression are very low, the problem of handling rutting stags is overcome. This process would also permit the deer to be selectively killed by spear or arrow.[17]

Biologists and archaeologists have not only asked why red deer were never domesticated but why, worldwide, so few of what would seem to be a vast array of ideal candidates for domestication actually made it as livestock or working animals.

Red deer in New Zealand being driven along a public road. Red deer have now been domesticated on New Zealand deer farms, disproving those archaeologists who said their domestication was impossible.

The most common response is that those species were tried, found wanting – for one reason or another – and discarded. Maybe there was some behavioural difficulty that prevented their exploitation. However, in the case of red deer in particular, that theory does not seem to bear water, for their domestication by New Zealand farmers during the twentieth century demonstrates that there are no serious problems innate in the species. Instead it seems rather that animals were only domesticated where there was a clear need for it. If there was a requirement to keep large numbers of male red stags permanently enclosed for their antlers, then one can well imagine that domestication would be neither desirable nor possible, at least until the advent of wire fences. If deer could be drawn to feed and then selectively killed, was there any point in attempting to further tame or domesticate them?

In suggesting why red deer were never domesticated, the eminent archaeologist Jean-Denis Vigne has proposed that this species had by the Neolithic been so important an object for hunters for so long that it had become virtually sacred as an animal of the hunt. As such, any attempts at taming or domestication would have been an unthinkable tabu.[18] I think there may be some merit in his idea. In many countries the notion of farming red deer has elicited very strong negative reactions among hunters, especially in Germany and Central Europe, where the hunting philosophy is especially strong. Those same hunters had no such scruples about fallow deer, which have existed in small parks throughout Germany for many years.

Hunting in parks was always understood to be an inferior sport, although Elizabeth I took delight in having park deer marshalled into paddocks so she could shoot them with a crossbow. As landowners became more urban, the idea of hunting in parks seemed even less attractive, and the killing of deer within the parks was delegated to servants. The elitism associated with the possession of deer parks seems to have transferred from the process of hunting to the meat itself. Venison was by association the token, the evidence for, and the ultimate association with, the hunting achievement. Gifts of venison remained laden with prestige and became more and more highly prized as the numbers of wild deer declined. This process was further accelerated in England by the introduction of an act making the sale of venison illegal in 1603. This was not rescinded until 1831. Venison had been a highly prestigious gift commodity for centuries, as demonstrated by the Royal Warrant whereby the monarch provided annual gifts of venison to the high and mighty from the thirteenth century until Margaret Thatcher, the British prime minister, put a stop to it during the 1980s.

In his diary Samuel Pepys recorded eating venison on 85 occasions between 1660 and 1668, compared to 50 mentions of beef. In all cases, the venison was either given to him as a haunch, a side of venison or when he was a guest at a meal, usually as a pasty. On several occasions, Pepys passed on the bounty he had received. He clearly deemed it a treat superior to the meat of domestic animals, and mentions two occasions when other meats were passed off as venison: in January 1660 he damns 'a [venison] pasty that was palpable beef which was not handsome' and in October 1661 'a venison pasty which proved a pasty of salted pork'. Reflecting the cachet of venison, the Royal Society, established in Pepys's lifetime, had in its original charter a clause that read: 'any nobleman or gentleman complimenting the company with venison, not less than a haunch, shall . . . be deemed an honorary member'.[19]

Whether fed to one's own guests or sent to those one wished to impress, or to grease a palm, venison, even as a gift, was a transient but very real asset. It didn't matter that it had been hunted by one's servants: indeed, that even reinforced its connotations of the power and prestige of the donor. By the eighteenth century, venison was so widely used by parliamentary candidates to influence potential voters that E. P. Thompson quipped: 'The deer must have dreaded a general election, unless they were, as good Whigs, anxious to contribute to constitutional stability.'[20]

4 Deer Hunting and Art

Allied to the distinction between wild and domesticated is the contrast between hunting and farming. It is significant that people have never devoted much time and effort to decorating agricultural tools, whereas the objects associated with hunting are almost always heavily decorated. Hunting has been so essential to our survival for so long that although it is no longer a part of our daily lives it seems reasonable to suppose that it remains deeply embedded in our psyches: fishing and hunting still remain sacred recreations. We all want to put 'gone fishing' on the door and lose ourselves in peace and quiet.

Ever since hominins arrived in Asia and Europe, perhaps as long as 1.8 million years ago, and encountered deer for the first time, we can suppose that these animals occupied a place in human culture as prized objects of the hunt. We know that much later, within Europe, Neanderthals were doughty hunters and that their methods entailed physical grappling with their prey, because the damage to their skeletons indicates that the injuries they sustained are similar to those of today's rugby players. Hunters ambushed migrating reindeer as they passed through the valleys of southwestern France, which furnished them with meat, fat, antler, bone, tendon and hides. As evidenced by the bone record, reindeer represented only 35 per cent of the kill in the Middle Palaeolithic, but this

Decorated hunting trousse, French, early 16th century, demonstrating the ceremonial importance of the ritual dismemberment of the deer carcase. Agricultural tools are never decorated in this way.

increased to 95 per cent in some sites by the Upper Palaeolithic, around 18,000 BP.

Directing migrating herds into suitable valleys and gullies to permit their being confined and killed must have required skilful organization, and it has been suggested that in the careful planning of the hunt may have lain the basis of the evolution of human language. Accurate prediction of the arrival of migratory animals was obviously of the utmost importance, and as reindeer movements are regular and largely unaffected by weather, perhaps it was this that motivated Upper Palaeolithic people to invent the lunar calendar.

As the reindeer moved north in the warming of the Holocene and their migrations became smaller, other prey species became more important. Of these, the red deer was pre-eminent. People continued to hunt reindeer and to follow them north, but they exploited the animals more and more as herders, establishing many independent tribes, each with its own individual culture. Reindeer were one of the very few large grazing mammals adapted to exploit this northern environment, from which the glacial megafauna had been hunted to extinction. Following the reindeer gradually became the established way of life for the people who inhabited the tundra and taiga. It is a way of life that still exists today.

As reindeer ranged further north following the retreating ice, red deer became the most utilized species in the majority of Eurasia. The exploitation of red deer was generally associated with the hunting of other species such as horses (the wild tarpan), aurochsen, roe and so on, but red deer remained the major contributor of meat throughout almost all European sites, as evidenced by the bone record.

In the long history of human interactions with deer, it is hunting that has been the principal point of connection. It is the hunt that has not only inspired almost all our art relating to deer, but has become one of the commonest subjects for our literature, myth and symbolism. Within that compass and across many cultures, it is deer that are the commonest and most esteemed quarry. This is as true now as it was 30,000 or many more years ago. The hunt, which for most of this long time span was the activity upon which human lives depended, has ingrained itself more deeply into humanity's pysche and subconscious than we realize.

Throughout the Mesolithic period and widely through Eurasia there are graves in which the tushes or canines of red deer have been found. They have often been painstakingly perforated by stone tools and worn as necklaces or other burial ornaments. In many places antlers have been found as grave goods, testimony to the value of red deer as the most important object of the hunt.

As for those in Asia, so for the first Americans, who continued to hunt deer after crossing the Bering Straits about 30,000 years ago. From Mexico to the far north, white-tailed deer, moose and caribou became, and remained, the staple source of meat until Europeans introduced cattle and virtually eliminated the deer, along with the buffalo.

Native Americans hunted deer in a great variety of ways, no doubt reflecting the skills and techniques used by Eurasians in prehistory. The Yokut tribe, for example, used decoys: either tame deer or a man disguised as a deer, wearing a stag's antlered head and sometimes painting himself white. Archaeologists at the Early Mesolithic site of Star Carr in North Yorkshire, England, also found a number of red deer skulls with antlers attached that had been cut in such a way as to suggest that they were designed to be worn by humans. The antlers had been deliberately trimmed to make them lighter while retaining their frontal

These 10,000-year-old antlers from Star Carr, Yorkshire, seem to have been carefully shaped to reduce their weight while retaining their profile, and the skull has been drilled to create eyeholes and presumably to permit the frontlet to be worn, either for shamanic purposes or to disguise a hunter approaching deer.

profile. It is unknown whether this was for shamanic ceremonies or for some form of hunting decoy.

Within the historic era, different hunting traditions developed. Not all methods entailed massive drives and such techniques as calling deer were also practised in Northern Asia, even by royalty. In China the Jurchen subjects of the Qidan paid part of their tribute to the Liao court in about AD 1000 by contributing experts who used horns to imitate the bugling of rutting deer. Even into the eighteenth century Manchu emperors employed specialists who dressed in deerskins and masks and called deer. The Mughals also used tame decoy antelope and deer for many years and the practice, not unlike that of the stalking horse, must have been widespread: there exists a thirteenth-century BC bronze dish from Kastamonu in Turkey dating to the Hittite imperial period which shows a hunter killing deer with a bow while holding a tame antlered deer on a lead, presumably a decoy.[1]

In Scotland narrow valleys were used as sites into which deer could be driven and ambushed; they became known as elricks and the body of beaters, the tainchell. In both Ireland and Scotland 'burnt mounds' exist beside the elricks. Although their purpose has not yet been confirmed, it is thought that these are the sites of stone troughs in which deer carcasses would be put with water; the carcasses could be boiled by throwing in hot

rocks, and the valuable fat could then be collected as the water cooled. The deeds of the hunters were commemorated in verse and the gatherings for these deer drives became the occasion of celebration with food and music.[2] Historical accounts of some of these survive, the most famous being that held for Queen Mary at Atholl in 1564, for which the Earl employed some 2,000 Highlanders to gather deer from the surrounding forests of Badenoch, Mar, Moray and elsewhere over a period of two months. Two thousand deer were estimated to have been collected and 360 deer, five wolves and some goats were killed at the gathering.[3]

One of the consequences of our dependence on hunting deer was the widespread incorporation of deer into shamanism. It was probably in this context that reindeer, elk and red deer became common subjects of the cave paintings and rock art of the Palaeolithic and Mesolithic throughout the whole of Eurasia. For most of this area, red deer and their relatives were the largest and most highly esteemed hunting quarry. Across the immensity of the steppes linking China and Europe other species intruded, particularly reindeer and elk in the north, but the red deer tribe were the staple quarry. Inevitably this spawned art. In Pictish carvings red deer are the most frequently featured animals after horses, while in Celtic mythology the god of fertility and wild animals, Cernunnos, 'the horned one',

This Roman mosaic depicts a tame stag being led off to the hunt (*opposite*) and, then in a separate scene the hunter prepares to shoot a second stag attracted to the first while the man leading the tame stag conceals himself. This graphically demonstrates a practice that was widespread in many cultures.

87

A Pictish stone
illustrating a
running deer
being seized
by a deerhound
or perhaps by
a wolf.

*Deer Dancers, Wild
Turkey Woman and
Buffalo Dancers,*
a Native American
ceremony held
in the southwest
in 1946. The
ceremony, still
danced by some
Puebloan peoples
in the USA, is
believed to have
been developed so
as to seek consent
from the hunting
spirit to kill deer
and to request
forgiveness from
the animals, and
perhaps also to
ask for good for-
tune in the hunt.

The Celtic god Cernunnos, 'the horned one', as depicted on the Gunderstrup cauldron probably made by Thracian craftsmen around 100–200 BC and recovered in pieces from a bog in Denmark.

is exquisitely represented in the Gunderstrup cauldron sitting cross-legged and wearing antlers that slightly resemble the stylized antlers of the steppe nomads. It has been suggested that Cernunnos may be linked to the Hittite Karhuhas, also a god of fertility.

For the Scythians and the nomads of the steppes, deer with characteristic stylized antlers became the hallmark of an entire and widespread civilization. Evolving from shamanism, closely associated with hunting and nomadic lifestyles, sprang the most important and visually exciting body of artifacts derived

89

One of 26 golden deer recovered from a burial mound near Filippovka, Southern Urals, dating from the 4th century BC.

from the representation of deer. This is the art of the nomads of the Eurasian steppes, a remarkably homogenous body of art reflecting cultures that covered a vast area over a long time period. In the West these art forms have been called Scythian and it is perhaps here that they reach their most magnificent stylized depictions of stags with exaggerated multi-pointed antlers. Prior to about 1,000 BC these peoples seem to have been more static, but, perhaps as a result of the development of cavalry, which gradually became prevalent from some point in the second millennium BC, their influence extended from Siberia and China to Scythia and the Carpathian mountains, almost from the Pacific to the North Sea, limited by no barriers other than the vast expanse of the grasslands themselves. Dependent initially on hunting and, later, grazing, their lives revolved around the horses they rode, the deer and ibex they hunted, the sheep, goats, cattle and camels they herded, the frogs, snakes and leopards they encountered and the eagles they used in falconry. These formed the background for a magnificently vigorous stylized animalistic tradition of sculpture, commonly in bronze, but occasionally using gold, silver and even, in the east, jade, as well as wood, bone, stone and other materials. Two-dimensional zoomorphic representations have survived on tattooed human skin preserved in frozen tombs in the Altai mountains, on leather and felt, and even in rugs.[4]

In addition the steppe nomads left behind them remarkable carved stone pillars, known as 'deer stones', and petroglyphs

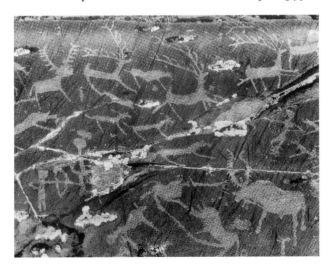

Mongolian deer stone, 2nd millennium BC. This Bronze Age rock art shows hunters armed with bows and arrows pursuing deer with hounds.

dating from before the Bronze Age (before 2,000 BC), when the deer depictions are more realistic, to the Late Bronze and Early Iron Age, when the animals are much more stylized. These stylized and static, often massive, deer were carved on standing stones that were first seen in the Transbaikal region of southern Siberia but have now been identified across north and central Mongolia and into the Altai region of Xinjiang province. Combinations of deer with figures of women giving birth have led some scholars to suggest that the deer are associated with regeneration. This would be typical of the symbolic role of deer in many cultures.

Because we have no record of their language, the meaning of the objects the steppe nomads left us remains fertile ground for conjecture. Deer images may have been expected to confer speed on a horse through being used in harness and saddle ornaments. Combat motifs in which a carnivore savages a herbivore might have been thought to symbolize power or to protect flocks from predators. Occasionally themes are assimilated from neighbouring non-nomadic cultures: for example, where deer or other ungulates are represented symmetrically around a tree or other vegetation, this is considered to be borrowed from Near Eastern iconography and to be associated with fertility.

For the surviving tribes of the northeast of Asia that may claim descent from the artists of this work, shamanism still remains a powerful force. The essence of southern Siberian shamanism is the flight of the shaman into the world of spirits borne on an antlered stag. Beating of the shaman's drum was supposed to echo the stag's heartbeats and the drum represented the stag, with its frame taken from a living consecrated tree symbolizing the Tree of Life, and the skin from a consecrated deer. The animal, despite its antlers, was female; hence the drumskin bore teats, while the shaman's robe was of deer-skin that had been prepared by women. Many Siberian shamans wore antler crowns that also incorporated representations of birds, reflecting the tradition that the shaman had been reared in the nest of an eagle.[5]

Siberian iron antler headpiece used by shamans.

The wearing of antler headpieces is certainly not limited to Siberian shamans. As we have seen from the antlered frontlets found at the early mesolithic site at Star Carr, the history of people wearing antlers is extremely ancient. The depiction of a figure known as 'the sorcerer' on the wall of the Trois-Frères cave near Ariège, France, from around 13,000 BC is sometimes taken to be that of a shaman wearing antlers. The Inuit of North America often use pieces of antler as charms and their shamans also frequently use antler headpieces. And the surviving Ainu people, who are Japan's first inhabitants and who historically survived by hunting deer, still wear antler head-dresses in their traditional dances. The same is true of the Bhutanese, who, a long way from Japan, use antler headpieces in their folk dances, although here the connection with shamans is less clear.

Imperceptibly, through the Neolithic, hunting became less important as a means of providing food. From about 10,000 years ago, cattle, sheep and goats gradually became more im-portant sources of meat within Europe. Antlers as a material for tools were superseded by bronze and iron. Shamanism gradually retreated north with the hunting communities.

Yet it seems that as the economic necessity for hunting declined, its ritual value grew. Hunting, at least when pursued by the nobility, followed closely prescribed rules and the hunting of deer increasingly became the preserve of the elite, who attempted to retain all deer for themselves by every avail-able means. Charlemagne created Frankish law to establish

Deer dancer, Bhutan. The mask dance of the Drametse community of Bhutan features 16 dancers wearing different masks representing mythical animals.

Wood carvings of paired red deer stags found in a ritual well shaft. This pair of Celtic wooden deer stags, dating from around 100 BC, are thought to have once decorated the well head of a well shaft in Baden-Württtenberg, Germany, in which they were found.

forests and deer parks in which he reserved deer for himself and other appointed grandees, and this concept spread through most of western Europe and persisted over many centuries; as, for example, in the Forest Laws of England introduced by William I and not wholly repealed until the nineteenth century.[6]

Further east, it was the Persians who appear to have first conceived the formal garden enclosed by a high wall and divided into four by canals intersecting at a pool. These they called *pairi-daeza*, meaning surrounded by a wall. The *pairi-daeza* often included, or were adjacent to, hunting parks. This word came into Europe as 'paradise' and the Latin word *parcus* descended from the same stem.

After conquering Persia, Alexander the Great absorbed much of the Achaeminid civilization, including the *pairi-daeza*, into Hellenic culture and diffused it widely. He himself was not above hunting in parks, as the Latin historian Curtius recounts in describing Alexander's exploits somewhere near Samarkand:

> Of the wealth of the barbarians in those parts, there are no greater proofs than the herds of noble beasts of the chase they keep shut up in great woods and parks. For this purpose they select extensive forests made pleasant by many springs of water that flow all year long. They surround the woods with walls and have towers as shelters for the hunters. For four successive generations, so it was agreed, the park had remained undisturbed. Alexander now entered it with his whole army and gave orders for the game to be driven from all directions.[7]

In England park deer occupied a strange legal position: as they had already been taken and possessed by the park owner, poaching them was considered theft. This does not seem to have deterred people from 'park breaking', as it was known, and from medieval times until the late eighteenth century park breaking, often by aristocrats pursuing vendettas against their neighbours, continued. Sometimes it reached epidemic proportions, emptying a park of all its deer.[8]

There was a regular trade in poached deer meat within England during the medieval period. Poaching must have been rife, because deer numbers declined over the centuries, reaching a nadir at the end of the eighteenth or beginning of the nineteenth century in Britain and probably through most of the rest of Europe. We know some minute details of poaching from the descriptions that survive of those convicted in the English forest courts. Snares were probably the commonest weapon in the medieval peasant poacher's arsenal.

The success of the poacher in challenging authority provided a rich seam in folklore across many countries.[9] There is a very close association between the legends of Robin Hood and the deer within the greenwood forest. Poaching of the deer, Robin's chief crime, and usually involved in his becoming an outlaw in the first place, 'outlawed for venison', was esteemed in these legends. Robin and his men often rescue poachers as they are about to hang, provide venison feasts, often for their unwitting prisoners, and so on. Occasionally Robin and his Merry Men break parks to steal deer, as from the Archbishop of York's park at Beverley in May 1323. Such legends, associated with outlaws stealing from the rich, often by poaching the rich man's deer, and then giving the booty to the poor, are of course universal, appearing almost to a formula in the folklore of most countries. The involvement of Robin Hood and his Merry Men with deer merely reflects the preoccupations of the medieval peasantry, for whom poaching was a regular and ongoing activity and for whom taking deer was felt to be a God-given right denied them by the king and nobility.

By the eighteenth century wild deer in England had almost vanished, yet deer parks, many of them belonging to bishops and the Church, were flourishing and the long-established 'sport' of park breaking was rekindled. The first and new Whig government under Walpole, nervous of Jacobites and determined to stamp out this threat to authority, introduced the draconian Black Act in 1723, consequently causing bewilderment among those awaiting execution who had considered that poaching deer was their right.[10] The Black Act made not only poaching, but offences against public order, property and much more, punishable by death.

In the May Day tradition, which seems to have pagan roots (and which the Church discouraged and the Puritans in New

Allegorical *Millefleurs* tapestry featuring deer and other animals, c. 1510.

England prevented), the King of May, variously known as the Lord of Misrule, the Summer Lord or the Abbott of Bon Accord, was gradually replaced by an actor called Robin Hood. Robin Hood figures carrying a bow and arrows and surrounded by forest imagery often led parades used to raise money in the fifteenth and sixteenth centuries. Such Robin Hood figures appeared from Aberdeen to the south of England and seem to represent anarchy. Yet such displays were sometimes incorporated into court ritual, as when 200 men dressed in green greeted Henry VIII and Catherine of Aragon in 1515; all released salvoes of arrows, then led the royal party to a bower in the woods and a venison breakfast.

Medieval folklore in England also includes the character of Herne the Hunter, famous because of his part in Shakespeare's

Merry Wives of Windsor. While Herne seems to be specifically associated with Windsor, little is known of him. He is probably merely a local representative of an international tribe of ghostly nightriders who participated in the Wild Hunt, and who were reputed to tear about in the dark and create mischief. In Germany they are associated with the cult of Wodan.

The folkloric tradition of wearing antlers was widespread and consistently opposed by the Church. Thus St Augustine in the fourth century condemned the 'filthy practice of dressing up like a horse or stag'. There is an association with the classical legend of Actaeon, who came upon Diana and her acolytes bathing while hunting, and was punished – rather harshly – by being transformed into a stag that was then killed by his own hounds. The widespread concept of the cuckold wearing horns may predate this legend or have developed from it. Actaeon was sometimes used as a cant name for a cuckold. There are other related myths, as in Ovid's *Metamorphoses*, in which Phoebe turns a knight into a stag. In folk tradition the notorious skimmington rides in which individuals were publicly humiliated included one in Devon where the shamed party, either a cuckold or a man who had been abused by his wife, was dressed as a stag and hunted by mounted huntsmen and lads dressed as dogs. This legendary event is referred to in Thomas Hardy's *The Mayor of Casterbridge* (1886).

The horn dance that still takes place every year in Abbots Bromley, Staffordshire, is a remarkable survival of the medieval rituals that were present in every village. Similar ceremonies were once common in Kent and known as Hoodening or hoddening. The dance is still performed faithfully in Abbots Bromley by ten men comprising six 'deer men', a fool, a hobbyhorse, a bowman and a Maid Marian. Collecting their antlers from the church in the morning and returning them in the evening, they dance a prescribed route all day. What is truly remarkable is that these antlers are reindeer antlers that have been carbon dated to around AD 1000.[11] Can they have come to Abbots Bromley with the Vikings? Why should the Vikings have brought reindeer antler headpieces from Scandinavia?

By the time of the first written accounts, hunting had become a recreation, but one that served a purpose. It was praised by the classical authors such as Xenophon in *Cyropaedia* and Oppian in *Cynegetica* as a means of rehearsal for war. Later, the medieval authors of the hunting manuals, principally French, extolled hunting as a means of combatting the lechery associated with lying abed.

In the East, royal hunts were an accepted way for rulers to demonstrate their power and administrative skills while moving around their kingdom with colossal and impressive entourages. In the eleventh century BC the Chinese Chengdi emperor purportedly used 11,000 troops to surround a mountain with a hunting net. The English traveller Thomas Herbert describes

Youths hunting deer on a Greek red figure cup, c. 500 BC. In this typically classical scene a red deer is being played with, suggesting a gladiatorial combat or bull fight, rather than a hunt.

game being enclosed by wire and cords supported by stakes requiring 600 camels to carry them in Safavid Iran in 1627–9. There are plausible accounts of beaters numbering between 10,000 and 100,000 on early hunts. These beaters were often mobilized for a month or more to drive game into an area of one to three miles in diameter, containing up to an incredible 10,000 assorted animals. Such spectacles served to aggrandize the ruler. They also developed an army that was accustomed to tight command and good coordination as well as long days of marching without sleep, since the line had to be held overnight: the beaters lit fires and bivouacked at close intervals to prevent game breaking back. Although Mongol riders were self-sufficient in carrying their own food and bedding, these hunts must also have provided a dress rehearsal for war in the organization of whatever stores and baggage trains there were.[12]

Even in England, Elizabethan kings and queens processed annually throughout the country, demonstrating their power

This painting by Giuseppe Castiglione (1688–1766) depicts the culmination of weeks of driving by the Chinese army to confine deer within a ring of horsemen so that Emperor Qianlong and his guests can hunt before an admiring public.

through the medium of the hunt. Deer were their principal quarry, not primarily for food but for their iconic value. The Greek classical myths of Diana and Actaeon became assimilated into medieval culture as symbols of Christ, regeneration and fidelity. Deer were prominent in foundation myths such as that of Holyrood Palace in Edinburgh and in the legends of St Hubert, St Eustace, St Giles and many others. As such, they were popular subjects for painters such as Pisanello, Dürer and Cranach. The last not only painted his aristocratic patrons but also hunting scenes featuring a series of seductive nudes accompanied by stags and roe bucks in a prelapsarian Garden of Eden, as Artemis or Diana, or as Cupid, or as characters in the Golden Age. Often the significance of these deer is unclear and some scholars have declared Cranach's deer to be 'semantically inert'. The artist was presumably exploiting his familiarity with deer and the obsessive enthusiasm of his patrons for deer and hunting. For most of those seeing his paintings, the presence of deer would immediately evoke wilderness and the forest, and their tameness would confirm the belief that before the Fall, man and animals, predator and prey, consorted in blissful harmony.

One of the most striking paintings of the early Renaissance in Europe is *The Hunt in the Forest* by Paolo Uccello, painted late in his life, around 1470. Uccello's reputation as a skilled user of mathematics and geometry to achieve complex perspectives is renowned and seems to suggest a calculated formality. However, in this painting he worked to a fairly simple pattern based on a central vanishing point. The vitality and movement are arresting. The subject is extremely unusual and somewhat puzzling, in that he depicts a roe deer hunt that appears to be taking place at night. Remnants of the original gold leaf placed on the trees convey an impression of moonlight, as does the canal or river on the right, and there is a faint crescent moon

Lucas Cranach the Elder, *Apollo and Diana*, 1526, oil and tempera on beech. Cranach was very familiar with deer due to the obsessive enthusiasm for hunting of his patrons.

Paolo Uccello's *The Hunt in the Forest*, c. 1470. This painting is highly unusual both in depicting a roe deer hunt and in implying that it took place at night using greyhounds, which hunt by sight.

discernible in the sky. The roe are being coursed by greyhounds and the hunters carry spears with which to deliver the *coup de grâce*. The crescent moon is a recurring motif on the bridles and reins of the many horses and presumably refers to Diana, goddess of hunting, whose emblem was the crescent moon. It seems unlikely that roe deer could be hunted during the night on horseback using greyhounds, which depend on sight to course the deer. Could it have been intended to represent the darkness that precedes a storm? That might relate to the chaotic scattering of the hunters.

European hunting manuals of the period precisely described the correct manner in which the hunt should be conducted, the hounds managed, and the deer dismembered and distributed. Poems such as *Sir Gawain and the Green Knight* and *Tristan and Isolde* confirm that the instructions were followed and demonstrate the depth of the symbolism. The hunting manuals were mostly written in French in the fourteenth and fifteenth century. Perhaps the most influential was that of Gaston Phébus, Count of Foix, who started to write his book on 1 May 1387. It was subsequently translated into English and adapted by Edward Duke of York around 1410. Both classical and medieval hunting manuals invariably mingle practical advice on the management of

the hounds and the correct procedure for the hunt with philo-
sophical points, and often extend into allegory.

Medieval tapestries and poetry drew on the chase as fertile
grounds for allegory. Thus the small fifteenth-century tapestry
in the Burrell Collection in Glasgow, woven in the north Rhineland and entitled *The Pursuit of Fidelity*, shows a couple sharing
a saddle as they chase a stag into a net. Apparently fidelity was
as elusive then as now.

One of the commonest images involving deer in European
art is of a stag bearing a cross between its antlers: the cruciferous stag. This image seems to have originated in the legend of
St Eustace but was subsequently adopted in the lives of Ss
Hubert, Theodore, Julian, Meinulph, Fantin, Felix of Valois and
others who were led to their conversion by a cruciferous stag.

The 15th-century
North Rhineland
tapestry *The Pursuit
of Fidelity* is an
allegory in which
the two riders do
their utmost to
capture Fidelity,
the stag, in a
net. Then, as
now, fidelity
seems elusive.

Pisanello, *The Vision of St Eustace*, c. 1440. Pisanello was very familiar with red deer (his patron was an obsessive hunter), thus the stag is painted so accurately as to be above criticism.

Nothing is known of the real person on whom the legend of St Eustace is based. It first appears in an eighth-century Greek work which thereafter was promulgated in Latin and most European languages, including English, over succeeding centuries.

In part one of the legend, 'the conversion', Placidas, a heathen but virtuous Roman general of the time of Trajan, is confronted with a beautiful stag while hunting. The stag leads Placidas away from his colleagues, then leaps onto an inaccessible rock, whence it turns to Placidas, who now sees between its antlers a vision of Christ being crucified. The stag asks Placidas why he is persecuting him, and is instructed to take his family to the bishop to be baptized.

Features of this legend are common to many such tales. Numerous species of animals have guided people to various destinations and fates throughout folklore. Several stags, often white, have guided medieval heroes across rivers: Clovis, Charlemagne and many others. The notion of a cruciferous stag guiding men to found abbeys is also widespread. David of Scotland, Henry the Lion of Germany, the Duke of Anségise, Ss Patrick and Giles, and Charlemagne himself all feature in such foundation myths, some of which involve white stags, some with and some without crucifixes.[13]

Hubert's legend was adapted from that of St Eustace in the fourteenth century and by the mid-sixteenth century had largely eclipsed that of St Eustace in artistic representations. Hubert was a real Bishop of Liége between 708 and 725 and is described as fierce and ungodly, a passionate hunter, until his encounter with the stag, when he was also given a stole by a descending angel and became virtuous. He became a cult figure attributed with the ability to prevent rabies. Throughout France, but especially in the Belgian village of St Hubert, hounds are still blessed annually in church on 3 November.

St Giles' legend differs from most of the others in that he protects a tame red deer hind, or in some images a roe doe, that has been wounded by a king. In legends associated with St Proculus, or the even earlier ones of St Aegidius, the hind supplies milk to sustain the saint. Similar legends associated with Irish saints are numerous.

It was not only among European cultures that rituals associated with the hunting of deer were prescribed. The Moche people, who inhabited the coastal strip of what is now northern Peru around the time of Christ and for six or seven centuries thereafter, ritualized the hunting of deer in ways that are not yet clearly understood. What we know is gleaned from their

Hunting the Deer for the Sacrifice, Native American artwork, undated, yarn on wood.

pottery, which is decorated with detailed fine line drawings. Although fish and fowl made up the main part of their diet, the depictions of hunting are restricted to sea lion and deer hunts. The killing of deer seems to have symbolized the human sacrifices central to their culture. In deer hunts the principal participants wore elaborate headdresses only seen in ritual contexts; they seem to have been members of the leading elite who also officiated in religious ceremonies. There are depictions of the deer trussed up in precisely the same way that the human captives were prepared for sacrifice and bloodletting. Presumably deer blood was consumed, and deer meat was eaten only at religious feasts and in the ceremonies associated with sacrifices.

The tradition of the massive ring hunts of China was carried through successive dynasties by the nomads as far west as the plains of eastern Europe. In Saxony and other German states the hunts evolved into 'holding hunts'. Teams of many hundreds of beaters would spend weeks driving game, principally deer and wild boar, into canvas walled corrals in which the animals could be systematically killed by crossbow. By the seventeenth century hunting in the German states entailed large numbers of beaters driving deer into lakes so the nobility could shoot them with crossbows. These are illustrated in great detail by Cranach, who, as the court painter of the Elector of Saxony, attended these hunts complete with his sketching panel. By the eighteenth century states were vying to produce more and more elaborate 'water hunts'. Rivers were diverted and lakes constructed on which were floated reconstructions of Venetian ships. These carried the hunters together with orchestras, to provide musical accompaniment specially composed by such eminent composers as Christoph Gluck. The terrified deer were driven through theatrical sets and forced to plunge into the water, where they made easier targets.

This German painting of a water-hunt accurately depicts a degrading spectacle in which red deer are driven through a wooden stage into water, where their slow swimming makes them easy targets for armed courtiers.

A contemporary account gives the flavour of these events:

> The Princes and their huntsmen, informed of the arrival
> of the Princesses on the boats by the firing of cannon,
> pursued the deer and forced it to break cover by the sound
> of the French horn. Twenty times or more it came to the
> shore and, frightened by the sight of the boats, retreated
> each time. Finally, chased by the hounds who were urged
> on by the huntsmen blowing their horns, it leapt into the
> water with the hounds swimming after it and surround-
> ing it. It immediately dived under the water and was lost
> from view, but soon reappeared and was again pursued
> by the hounds. The more it defended itself the more it
> was attacked; this struggle lasted almost an hour and
> provided endless enjoyment. The horns sounded in turns
> during this time, the deer finally fought its last battle and
> the huntsmen proclaimed its death. Four gondolieri then
> seized the deer by its antlers and dragged it on board,
> where it immediately perished.[14]

Enormous hunting palaces were built from which hunts could
be launched. Of these, Moritzburg near Dresden was perhaps
the most renowned. The deer were fed and managed in the parks
of these castles and it is here that the concept of antler trophies
seems to have developed from the vogue of the curiosity cabi-
nets, or Kunstkammer, which emerged in the mid-sixteenth
century. Focussing initially on diseased and malformed antlers,
attention soon moved to growing and collecting stags with the
the largest trophies, establishing a trend that now extends worldwide and is the basis of a substantial industry.

By the end of the eighteenth century the numbers of deer in
Britain had reached a nadir. They were almost extinct in England,

where roe had probably disappeared; red deer survived only in pockets in the southwest and possibly in Cumbria. Fallow continued in the surviving parks and as escapees, but were not popular quarries for hunts.

As a result, there came a vogue for hunting the carted stag. Hunts established paddocks usually adjacent to their kennels in which small herds of red deer were bred with the specific object of carting them up and taking them off to the hunt meets. When the stag, or sometimes a hind, was run to bay it would be put back in the cart and returned to the paddock to hunt another day. Such deer became named celebrities, and many ran several hunts a year for several years. With the advent of faster horses that could be jumped, fox hunting became more attractive than hunting carted deer, but at their height the carted

The carted stag 'Winchelsea' painted by William Barraud in 1844 is shown being released from his cart which is being driven away, to be ready to collect him when he eventually stands to bay. This renowned stag once ran along the main London–Brighton railway line and into a tunnel with the hounds behind him and a train at the rear. All emerged unscathed.

hunts in England numbered 130. Some survived well into the twentieth century.[15]

When Queen Victoria married Prince Albert of Saxe-Coburg and Gotha they travelled to Scotland. Albert, who had hunted chamois and deer in Germany, was encouraged to hunt Scottish red deer, killing two tame stags by shooting them from the dining-room window of Atholl Castle. He was also placed in suitable positions for shooting deer as they were driven past him. First William Scrope in 1822 then St John in 1832 and Augustus Grimble, who published his *Deer Stalking* in 1886, and many others visited Scotland to hunt deer and write about it with great enthusiasm.[16] Soon the Scottish sport of stalking deer – approaching them by stealth, against the wind, until close enough to take the shot – became highly fashionable. Initially

HILL & SMITH,

BRIERLEY HILL, NEAR DUDLEY.

BRANCH DEPOTS— { 118 QUEEN VICTORIA STREET, LONDON.
{ 47 DAWSON STREET, DUBLIN.

CONTINUOUS DEER PARK FENCING, No. 7.

THIS fence is recommended as the best Deer Fence yet introduced for durability, appearance, or economy. It is easily fixed in curved or undulating lines, and may at any time be taken up and refixed. It requires no side-stays, wood, or stone blocks, nor is any excavation required in its erection, yet its firmness and rigidity when fixed are such that, after many years' experience, in many deer parks in England, it is found in as good a state as when first erected.

It is 6 feet high above ground and 18 inches below, the standards being placed 3 feet 9 inches apart; size of joining standards, $1\frac{3}{4}$ in. × $\frac{3}{8}$ in., and of intermediate ones, $1\frac{1}{2}$ in. × $\frac{3}{8}$ in. It has eight bars, the top one round, $\frac{3}{4}$ in. diameter, joined in every fourth standard by means of H. & S.'s improved ferrule joint, and the others flat iron, 1 in. × $\frac{1}{8}$ in., placed edge upwards, and connected by means of H. & S.'s overlap joint, as before described. Small holes are made in the lower space of all the standards, in order that, should it be found necessary, wires may at any time be added to prevent fawns creeping through. The fence is much improved by the addition of an extra horizontal bar.

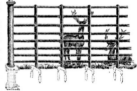

PRICES.

	At Works.	Delivered in London or 100 Miles on any Railway.	Delivered in Glasgow or Dublin.
With 8 Bars	3/-	3/5	3/6 a yard.
,, 9 ,,	3.2½	3/7½	3/9 ,,

STRAINED WIRE FENCE FOR DEER PARKS, No. 23½.

STRAINED WIRE FENCE, No. 23½.

THIS fence for the enclosure of deer is a cheap, elegant, and efficient substitute for either stone walls or wood fencing. It is 6 feet high above ground and 18 inches below, the 6-feet standards having alternately triangular and pronged feet as represented, and placed 9 feet apart, the size of the iron being $1\frac{1}{2}$ in. × $\frac{3}{8}$ in. Between these standards are placed shorter ones sufficiently high to take in five wires, thus preventing the deer creeping through the fence, the size of the shorter standards $1\frac{1}{4}$ in. × $\frac{3}{8}$ in. In the lower half of the fence, therefore, the standards are only $4\frac{1}{2}$ feet apart. The wires are 10 in number, the six upper ones No. 4, and the lower ones No. 6 gauge, in long lengths, and of the best prepared quality of solid wires, or galvanized strand wire, as may be preferred. The straining pillars are cast-iron, of an octagon shape, with ornamental caps, are prepared to fix on stone, and are placed 100 yards apart, each having a strong double stay.

Price, including one straining pillar only per 100 yards, **2/9** per yard with solid wires, delivered free at any railway station, including everything except stones for the straining pillars; or, if fixed by H. & S. complete, **6d.** per yard extra, the proprietor providing two assistant labourers.

If with galvanized strand wires of same sizes, which are strongly recommended, instead of solid wires, the price is **3/-** per yard delivered, with the same additional for fixing.

A 17th-century carved stag eating a turnip. The turnip may indicate that the hunter had fed a stag on his land all winter, or perhaps there was some thought of the stag needing to enjoy its last bite, or maybe it is an allusion to dittany.

the stalkers worked with hounds to course the wounded stags but later, as firearms improved, the dogs were dispensed with. Following royalty, a great vogue began for those in England to take the train north to a hunting lodge in Scotland for a late summer season. A vast number of oil paintings of the Scottish glens and their deer were painted to remind the sportsmen of their adventures. Landseer's *Monarch of the Glen*, painted for the dining room at the House of Lords in 1851, was pre-eminent among these. It is now the property of the multinational drinks company Diageo, and is without question the most recognized and reproduced painting of deer. It has been used and abused in countless advertising campaigns. Deer stalking is still important to Scotland's economy, bringing in an estimated £105 million per annum, and creating valuable employment in rural areas.

Some of the ancient traditions of hunting persist, and this is nowhere more true than in Germany and Central Europe, where hunters who inadvertently transgress the unwritten code of correct conduct are still subject to good-humoured corporal punishment. It is, for example, *de rigeur* for those who have killed deer to place some greenery in their mouths. The origin of this is not very clear. Modern hunters usually say that they wish to give the deer some taste of its last food on earth to help it into the next life, or to express gratitude to the deer for letting them shoot it. Historically there is a long tradition of deer curing themselves of hunting injuries, even shedding an embedded arrow, or of cleansing themselves of venom after killing snakes, by eating dittany. Dittany is a herb but its precise identity remains an enigma. There are many wooden carvings of deer in Germany with vegetation in their mouths. Whether this is related to modern hunting tradition is unclear.

Often, also in Germany, deer antlers were mounted on carved wooden heads, since presumably in years gone by this was simpler than relying on taxidermy, then an undeveloped art. In Britain such heads survive – at Hampton Court Palace, for example, or at Falkland Palace in Fife – but in Germany they are ubiquitous. Occasionally those carved heads are sculpted with a turnip in the stag's mouth. Again, opinions are divided as to the significance of this. It has been suggested that the turnip was put in if the stag had been shot by the farmer on whose land the deer had spent its life feeding. Perhaps this is related to the dittany story.

Evolving from the German interest in trophies came systems of measuring antlers that permitted hunters to compare trophies. In Europe an organization now called the International Council for Game and Wildlife Conservation created the CIC rating, while in North America and other parts of the world the Safari Club

International (SCI) use their own grading system. These two systems remain the most used and annually publish listings of record trophies. Inevitably large male deer with big antlers have become highly valued and attract substantial sums of money. In the USA some white-tailed bucks have sold for $1 million, although this probably takes account of possible sales of frozen semen. Hunting has come a long way from the deer drives.

5 Deer as Symbols

Mankind's intimate involvement with deer since prehistory has created a rich seam of myths and symbols that furnish our art and literature. Most are based on human observation of a large animal briefly glimpsed vanishing into the deep forest in the grey dawn, leading its own life independent of human agency. Such transient observations are fertile ground for myth and for confirming preconceived ideas. Thus we find symbolism, myth and legend associated with deer as objects of the hunt; as lusty animals rutting violently; as stags walking purposefully and apparently inexplicably on their migrations to their rutting stands; as animals with large ears alert and listening; as mothers fondly tending their young; as roe deer in a family group; as red deer having an affinity with water, in which they swim strongly, and into which they run when pursued by hounds or when wounded; as existing in the confines of a park; perhaps as sneezing and snorting when expressing parasites from their nose; as having a strange gland in front of their eyes; as occasional white red deer; and even simply as wild and mysterious creatures onto which apparently baseless symbolism can be attached.

Many 'attributes' of the stag were frequently repeated over centuries – the weeping stag, the collared stag with or without wings, the drinking stag, stags swimming, eating snakes and so

A trace of part of the carved stone font at Melbury Bubb church in Dorset, which was originally the base of an Anglo-Saxon cross. Its depictions include a stag eating a serpent: good overcoming evil. After ingesting the venom the stag would seek water or perhaps eat the herb dittany to cleanse and purify itself.

on – but the meaning of these various images is variable over time and place, sometimes making them difficult to decode, especially without a clear historical context. Nevertheless many of these seemingly unrelated attributes of the stag were in fact linked in the minds of those using the images. The common thread is their representation as symbols of time, longevity, endurance and regeneration, associated with the casting and regrowth of antlers. In the same way, snakes that were seen to renew their skins were also symbols of renewal.[1] As uniquely deciduous organs, antlers especially came to symbolize regeneration across many cultures and often to provide a *vade mecum* for all debilitating disease, including impotence.

It is no accident that most Eurasian symbolism is associated with red deer, especially the adult male hart or stag. Fallow were debased by the familiarity and constraints of the park, and the small roe deer were much less impressive. European monarchs and aristocrats wished to be associated with the elite red deer and attempted to reserve the hunting of them for themselves. This animal is without doubt the acme of deer-related symbolism in European literature, and has become so charged with cultural baggage that it eclipses any other animal within its European context.[2]

Deer were loaded with symbolism from the earliest time and across disparate cultures. A remarkable series of objects have been recovered from tombs of the Tang period in China, about 4,000 years ago. Consisting of wooden sculptures surmounted by antlers, these are assumed to have been created as tomb guardians, symbolizing renewal and longevity. Some of the sculptures incorporate cranes, which carried a similar symbolic value, and some have enormous tongues carved on to stylized faces. The extraordinary concentration on the tongue

Chinese Tang dynasty antlered grave guardians with long tongues. Several of these wooden sculptures erected to guard tombs in the 5th to 2nd century BC have survived in southern China. The antlers are usually decorated and the woodwork painted. The elongated tongue may emphasise the power of speech.

in these tomb guardian figures seems completely inexplicable and bizarre to the modern eye.[3]

A much later royal sceptre recovered from the ship burial at Sutton Hoo in southeast England, dating from about AD 625, is probably associated with the East Anglian king Raedwald. The balance of opinion now is that the sceptre is pre-Christian Celtic in style, and is possibly the work of Scottish craftsmen. The main body of the enigmatic sceptre is a four-sided stone bar 58 cm long, which can be recognized as a whetstone for sharpening weapons or tools, but at the top is a finial consisting of a bronze ring surmounted by a bronze stag with exaggerated antlers. As a sceptre the association with kingship is obvious and it has been argued that the long, delicate whetstone symbolized the tongue and the importance of oratory for any ruler.[4] If correct, this notion could cast light on the role of the tongues of the Chinese tomb guardians.

The associations between antlered stags and kingship and most especially with dynastic renewal became the key element in the iconography of the stag in Europe. The Swedish hero Beowulf defends the mead hall of King Hrothgar of the Danes from the demon Grendel in the Anglo-Saxon epic poem *Beowulf*. This hall is named the Heorot, or Hall of the Hart, and may have carried stag's heads on each gable.

There seems to be a clear connection between legends of deer and the foundation of dynasties, and this is further strengthened by two other cases in which deer are involved in dynastic conflicts. The first is that of Sertorius' deer in Plutarch, in which a fawn caught hunting is used by Sertorius to claim a link with Diana and so help him subdue superstitious tribes. Second is Sylvia's pet stag, which, when wounded by Ascanius, provokes a conflict between the Trojans and the indigenous people of Latium that will decide the imperial destiny of Rome.

Early 7th-century
sceptre from the
Sutton Hoo ship
burial in Suffolk.
Probably Celtic,
the sceptre (a 55
cm whetstone) is
surmounted by
a bronze stag
symbolizing
royalty. It has
been suggested
that the whetstone
symbolizes the
tongue and was
there to whet the
ruler's oratory.

In the earliest written texts deer are linked to longevity. Thus Hesiod, translated by Ausonius, gives a verse from 'the Precepts of Chiron':

Three times two and nine times ten complete the sum of years attained by men who reach their allotted span. Nine times the chattering crow exceeds this lifespan, and the stag passes through four times the lifespan of the crow.

Hesiod was one of the earliest Greek poets, and this proverb associating the stag with longevity has influenced Western literature and the visual arts from the very earliest times. Plutarch, Oppian and Pliny, albeit rather sceptically, repeated the notion, and it is also referred to by Cicero, Horace and other classical authors. Ovid rejuvenates Medea with a potion containing a stag's liver and parts of a crow 'more than nine generations old'.[5]

Refreshingly Aristotle introduced some common sense and a more reasoned approach to the longevity of deer:

Fabulous stories are told concerning the longevity of the animal, but the stories have never been verified, and the period of gestation and the rapidity of growth in the fawn would not lead one to attribute extreme longevity to this creature.

In fact, hinds do well to live to fifteen years and the stag twelve.

Ausonius and others extended their account of *The Ages of Animals* by introducing the raven and other elements and using these to compute the age of the universe. This cosmology forms the basis of the extraordinary tessellated pavement before the high altar in Westminster Abbey, which was created in 1268 by

Italian craftsmen known as *cosmati*. It was in the centre of this pavement that English monarchs were anointed with holy oil. The pavement was designed to convey mysticism, solemnity and importance to the occasion as well as to symbolize the longevity of the ruler and the dynasty.[6]

Even today, 'Is it true that you can tell the age of a stag from the number of points on its antlers?' remains one of the commonest questions directed at people who work with deer, though the answer is a resounding no. The myth features in Pliny the Elder's *Natural History* and has recurred and been adapted ever since. In a fifteenth-century miniature illustrating poems by Henri Baude, for example, two stags are being hunted. One is a winged stag representing Louis XI, with 40 points for his 40 years, and the other signifies the young Dauphin, with twenty points.[7]

Rather in the same way that emparking deer conveyed possession and status over many generations, so, it seems, did catching red deer stags or harts and placing collars round their necks.[8] This strange practice was very widespread and persisted for many centuries. Pliny's *Natural History* records that stags bearing golden collars, placed around their necks by Alexander the Great, had been found 100 years after his death. There are many other examples of the finding of collared stags many decades after the lifetime of the person who apparently attached the collar. Possibly the earliest, according to Michael Bath, is that recorded by Pausanias, who describes the 'sacred deer of the Mistress', Despoina, in Arcadia, bearing a collar with the words: 'I was a fawn when Agapenor was at Troy.' As Agapenor was the Homeric leader of the Arcadians, it has been suggested that this deer provides a link with the foundation of the Arcadian dynasty and follows another very early legend that links a collared stag to the founding of Greek settlements in Apulia.

There are English legends of stags being found with collars round their necks. One described by John Ray in 1661 recounts a traditional tale of a stag bearing a brass collar inscribed: 'When Julius Caesar here was king/Round my neck he put this ring/Whosoever doth me take/Let me go for Caesar's sake.' And Nicholas Upton in the fifteenth century described a stag that was killed in Windsor Forest at Besastine near Bagshot, with a gold collar inscribed: 'When I was a little deer/Caesar put this collar here.'

Michael Bath refers to the Robin Hood plays of Anthony Munday, which, printed in 1601, argue keenly for the divine right and legitimate succession. They describe Richard I killing a stag bearing a collar inscribed 'When Harald Harefoote raigned king,/ About my necke he put this ring.' A noble explains a legend in which the fleetfooted king is reputed to have run a stag down and 'collared' it. Since Harald Harefoot was the successor to Canute in 1037 and it was Harold I who is credited with uniting England into one kingdom, then dynastically it is very appropriate that he should have been so honoured.

In Germany Count Palatine Frederick IV also placed a brass collar on a red stag; the collar still exists and is inscribed: 'Dear hunter let me live. The Elector gave me freedom 1609.'

Napoleon reputedly netted a large stag in the forest of Vincennes in 1808 and in honour of Empress Josephine had it fitted with a gilded bronze collar inscribed in German 'The empress Josephine gave this stag its life on 8th September 1808.' The stag was allegedly retaken in 1836 – a pretty improbable life span for a stag, even if not up to some of the other legendary lives of stags. That it was not longer may reflect how short-lived was the Napoleonic dynasty.

In Denmark there is a stuffed red deer stag in the hunting museum at Horshølm near Copenhagen which is said to show

Hoc Cæſar me donauit.

The winged and collared stag emblem of French royalty adopted from the legend of Caesar collaring stags.

the marks of a collar. This stag has been in the Royal Collection since 1691 and it is considered that it may actually be the remains of an animal that once bore a collar signifying the dynastic revival of the absolute monarchy of King Frederick IV of Denmark. I have been to the excellent museum at Horshølm and examined this stag, including an x-ray of it. It is an amazing, if to modern eyes rather clumsy, piece of early taxidermy, no doubt dating to the late seventeenth century. However, I was not at all convinced by the mark round its neck. It seemed to me that the technique of taxidermy, revealed in x-rays, whereby pieces of deer skin had been tacked to a wooden frame could account for the line around its neck. In addition, we know the precise place the collar sits on the neck in farmed deer: if loose, it slides towards the chin when the animal grazes, and if tight, it gravitates to the same position, since it is the place where the neck has the narrowest girth. This did not correlate with the marks on the stuffed stag at Horshølm.

In Germany in Lübeck cathedral, there is an inscription describing how Charlemagne collared a stag that was hunted and killed 400 years later by Henry the Lion, Duke of Saxony, who built the cathedral on that spot. He is pictured aiming his bow at a collared stag with a crucifix between its antlers. Michael Bath considers this to be a basic foundation legend 'with pious accretions' gleaned from the legend of St Eustace.

In England, in 1611, the Landgrave Otto came to the court of James I to woo Princess Elizabeth and is documented as having placed a collar on a fallow buck on 30 July. Bath points out that this could very well have been a 'comment on the dynastic implications of the Landgrave's proposed royal marriage' and the hopes for 'cementing a Protestant alliance that would balance the continuing power of the Empire'.

In many legends the collar on the deer is reputed to have been placed there by Caesar and this forms the basis for Petrarch's love sonnet (Rhyme 190) in admiration of Laura. In it, Laura is represented by a white hind who cannot be taken because she is dedicated to Caesar. The hind is pure because she is white, while her collar symbolises fidelity and chastity. Petrarch's sonnet was the inspiration for many poems including the famous one by Sir Thomas Wyatt that is sometimes considered to have been directed at Anne Boleyn, with Henry VIII as her Caesar:

Who list her hunt, I put him out of doubt,
As well as I, may spend his time in vain.
And graven with diamonds in letters plain

There is written her fair neck round about:
'*Noli me tangere*, for Caesar's I am,
And wild for to hold, though I seem tame.'

The phrase '*Noli me tangere*' is, of course, usually associated with the resurrected Christ's admonition to Mary in the Garden of Gethsemane. Perhaps Wyatt is exalting the fair woman by making a veiled reference to her divinity.

Up to the Renaissance it was accepted that the legends of collared stags, their longevity, and the age of a stag being reflected in the number of points on their antlers were received opinions whose actual veracity was assumed. Thereafter the legends became literary and artistic devices for communication between cognoscenti and were used by Erasmus, Shakespeare, Donne and others. By the eighteenth century scepticism was in order but the stag retained its value as an emblem, while the proverb of the oldest animals and the notion of its longevity as propounded by Hesiod persisted in Scottish and Irish Gaelic until modern times. Other versions existed in Wales, Spain, Portugal, Venice, Belgium and Germany.[9]

An unusual example of a stag being used to confer dynastic legitimacy is the massive painting in the National Gallery of Scotland entitled *Alexander III of Scotland rescued from the Fury of a Stag by the Intrepidity of Colin Fitzgerald, ancestor of the present Mackenzie Family*. Painted in 1786 by the American-born Benjamin West, it was commissioned by the future Lord Seaforth, who claimed lineal descent from Colin Fitzgerald. Legend has it that after rescuing his king, Colin was granted the lands of Kintail, including Eilean Donan castle, seen in the background. Having lost their title and lands as a result of their support for the Jacobites in 1715 and 1719, the family became Hanoverian supporters in the 1745 and were rehabilitated.

A folio from the English 'Tudor Pattern Book', c. 1520s. Books illustrating animals were for centuries invaluable sources for artists who may have had no opportunity to see the original.

This commission therefore represents an attempt to have the Mackenzies' reputation as loyal subjects reinforced.

In France in his year of accession, 1380, Charles VI is reputed to have taken a collared stag bearing the inscription 'Caesar gave this to me.' The king was so moved that he had the stag released, but thereafter took a winged collared stag as the French royal badge and had this perpetuated in his royal furnishings and metalwork. Astonishingly the story is given some credence, for there exists a documented record in the royal accounts of a payment made to one Colin le Serrurier for a *fleur de lis* with which a stag, caught and housed in 1382, was to be branded before being released. In a prophecy dating to the period of the accession of the young Charles VI, Philippe de Mezières portrays Charles as *le cerf volant couronné* who will recreate

Charlemagne's empire. The identification of the young king in this way became an established part of French literature at the time as he was figured defeating France's enemies and leading France into a new empire.

From as early as the mid-fourteenth century, some decades before Charles VI's capture of the collared stag, France had used a large wooden statue of a stag wearing a shield around its neck to decorate the Palais Royal. However, in 1389 a more than life-size articulated wooden stag, painted white and bearing the French heraldic arms around its neck, although not winged, was created for the entrance of Isabelle of Bavaria to Paris. This lay on a bed, the *lit de justice*, near the Chatelet. A concealed operator could make it roll its eyes and move its mouth and limbs so that it could wave a sword at the passing queen, and also participate

Benjamin West, *Alexander III of Scotland Rescued from the Fury of a Stag by the Intrepidity of Colin Fitzgerald ('The Death of the Stag')*, 1784–6, oil on canvas.

in an allegorical tableau. Such complex articulated models were the preserve of craftsmen from the East who had travelled throughout Europe during the fourteenth century. Subsequently mechanical stags now fitted with wings, *cerfs volants*, including one 7.5 m high, became regular participants in French royal ceremonial. After being a symbol of longevity and then of imperial renewal, in France, the stag, now equipped with wings, became associated with the *lit* as a symbol of justice from the beginning of the fifteenth century. The winged stag, *le cerf volant*, bearing a characteristically crown-shaped golden collar of *fleurs-de-lis*, then remained Charles VI's own badge until his death. Until well into the sixteenth century it was the recognized badge not only of French royalty but also of French justice, while retaining its association with longevity and imperial renewal.[10]

The winged, collared stag of France reached Scotland when James V of Scotland married Mary of Guise. At Linlithgow Palace, the birthplace of their daughter Mary, Queen of Scots,

Winged stags as icons of justice forming a tympanum above the entrance to the Palais de Justice, Rouen, now in the Musée des Antiquités, Rouen, 15th century.

The winged stags of France appear at Linlithgow Palace in Scotland in roof bosses and, as here, on the fountainhead of the well. They were placed to mark the marriage of James V to Mary of Guise in 1538.

and one of James's most favoured palaces, there remains a fountain erected in 1538 which carries the royal arms of France impaling those of Scotland. The palace also features roof bosses bearing winged stags.

From the late fifteenth century, winged stags often wearing crown shaped collars were widely used as heraldic supporters and the motif was also taken up during the sixteenth century

The Colquhoun crest above the main gates of Rossdhu House on Loch Lomond, Scotland. Rossdhu is home to the chiefs of the Clan Colquhoun.

as a mark by French printers and was revived by the Dutch printer, Herman Borculous at the end of that century.[11]

The Bourbon duke Pierre II adopted the winged stag as the Bourbon motif, associated with the motto 'Esperance'. In 1515, when Francois I passed through Lyon en route to reclaiming Milan and Lombardy for France, Charles, Connétable de Bourbon, laid on elaborate festivities. In one of the tableaux a winged white stag directed by the Connétable, who was bearing a flaming sword and standing on its back, pulled figures representing the king and queen in a ship across the river and presumably on to total victory in the forthcoming campaign. This recalled the legend by which a deer guided Clovis across the river Vienne in his campaign against the Germans, while in other versions the stag was white and guided Charlemagne across, variously, the Gironde or the Rhine.

The winged stag was not Charles VI's only badge. He also used a collar of 'broom-cods', the seedpods of the broom or Genista plant (*genet* in French). Thus when Richard II of England married Charles VI's daughter, Isabella, in 1396, he gave Charles his device of a badge of a white hart, which he had first given to his supporters in 1390 at the October tournament at Smithfield. In return he received the *plants à genet* device that was also current in the French court, even though it had been the mark of the Plantagenets in England for 200 years by that time. Richard's use of the white hart wearing a crown collar and a gold chain as his badge probably reflects the use by his mother, the Fair Maid of Kent, of a white hind, and by his half-brother, the Earl of Kent, of a hind lying beneath a tree. However, the English Royal Wardrobe Book states that in 1393 a payment was made to John Shelwode for keeping a white hart in Windsor Forest. There is also a strange legend that Richard II was saved from a white stag by Herne the Hunter, presumably in Windsor.

The reverse of the right-hand panel of the Wilton Diptych, c. 1395, illustrating the badge of Richard II.

In the enigmatic Wilton Diptych in the National Gallery, London, almost certainly painted for Richard ii in or after 1395, we see both of these badges repeated many times. The white hart appears on the kneeling Richard's mantle and on the left shoulder of each of eleven angels, and it occupies the entire reverse of the right-hand panel. The Diptych served to enforce Richard's dynastic status.

In English history there is also the legend of Henry iii sparing the life of a white hart that was subsequently killed by Thomas de la Lynde in the Vale of Blackmore, Dorset. His family were then required by the King to pay a fine in perpetuity. The story features in Thomas Hardy's *Tess of the D'Urbervilles* (1891) and the fine, 'White Hart Silver', was paid from the thirteenth century till the reign of Victoria.

Another instance of royalty valuing white deer for its association with dynastic legitimacy features James i of England, who in 1621, on hearing that a white hind had been seen during a deer drive on Rannoch Moor in Scotland, attempted to have the animal captured. An English forester called John Scavander was despatched to catch her but returned empty-handed.[12] James may have been motivated by his Scottish background, since there is a long tradition in Scotland that the sight, but most especially the death, of a white red deer presages some calamity in the ruling household, normally a death. One of the MacLeod chiefs is reputed to have had a man executed for killing a white stag.

As we have seen here and in other contexts, the white hart or stag is especially laden with symbolic significance. This is not surprising. Although white fallow deer are commonplace, reflecting a high degree of inbreeding, white red deer are much rarer. They are not albinos but have occurred spontaneously throughout history, particularly on islands or in parks where a degree

A White Hart Inn sign. This is based on the badge of Richard II of England who was the monarch under whom inns were first licensed, although this inn is in Scotland at Edinburgh, and seems to be a post-1707 union token of loyalty to the new British government.

of inbreeding increases the chance of white deer being born. Their very rarity no doubt added to their symbolic value. In the same way the white whale, Moby-Dick, or the white rabbit in *Alice in Wonderland*, carry mystical values – in particular, causing the person who sees them to follow them and often become changed. It is no surprise that white harts became Richard II's badge and one of the most popular names for public houses, for in 1393 Richard passed an Act requiring inns to carry signs. Occasionally red deer carry a white blaze and this is reflected in the pub name The Bald Headed Stag.

The importance attributed to the white stags is also reflected in their popularity within coats of arms, especially as heraldic supporters.

So far we have considered the secular symbolism of the stag in Western Europe, but the stag as used in Christian texts and art is perhaps even more powerful and widespread. From the classical authors came observations of natural phenomena, albeit frequently mythical. Some, such as longevity, we have already discussed. Many others existed and many made their way into biblical texts: thus it was assumed that the stag is swift-footed, lustful, timid yet curious, susceptible to being charmed by music, and keen of hearing when its ears are erect but not when they are lowered. When wounded by arrows he can eat dittany, which causes the arrows to fall out and the wounds to heal; stags swim in a line, each resting his head on the rump of the one in front; stags eat snakes and, according to Oppian's *Cynegetica*, then rush to water in order to cleanse themselves of the venom and refresh themselves. Oppian also describes the infra-orbital glands of the stag as second nostrils that exude a waxy substance, later confused with Bezoar stone, believed to be a prized remedy against poison.

The notion of the snake-eating propensity of deer seems to have come from the East, as evidenced by Islamic texts, and Sassanian and Indian art. I have already mentioned the association of snakes with regeneration because they were seen to cast their skin. In the same way stags cast their antlers. This may have been a factor in the link between stags and snakes. Stags were supposed to eat snakes, and it has been suggested that this idea may have arisen thanks to observations of deer putting their noses to the ground and snorting and sneezing when they are expelling the larvae of the nasal bot.

St Augustine, in commenting on Psalm 41, used this story in a sermon delivered around AD 414 in which he drew on the stag as symbolizing swiftness but also for killing snakes, after which it runs impetuously to quench its thirst in streams. 'The snakes are your sins; destroy the serpents of sin, and then you will more keenly long for the fountain of truth.' Augustine also used the image of swimming stags resting their heads on the one in front to illustrate the text: 'Bear ye one another's burdens, and

A carved capital from the 12th-century priory at Serrabone, Languedoc. A centaur shooting a stag is a common motif in French Romanesque art. The centaur might stand for the Devil firing arrows of desire, while the stag represents good and perhaps even Christ.

so fulfil the law of Christ.' Augustine used these texts although there is no reference to them in the Bible.[13]

I had always rubbished the notion of stags swimming in line but recently I was talking to a long established fish-farmer on the west of Scotland who told me that he had seen five stags swimming strongly in line ahead some distance out to sea.

St Jerome similarly used the metaphor of the stag destroying evil things before thirsting and seeking out pure water in which to wash and renew itself. These commentaries relating to Psalm 41 explain why stags are commonly found on fonts, often in the company of the four rivers of paradise and the Mound and Tree of Life, as well as snakes. Communion wafers were occasionally stamped with a stag to signify the renewal associated with communion. Bede followed Augustine but took the comparison a stage further in identifying the stag as an image of Christ. This image remained a powerful motif for centuries.[14]

The illuminated initial letter Q found in the St Albans Psalter for Psalm 41 illustrates a stag devouring a snake. This tale is not present in biblical texts at all but was introduced to Christian mythology from classical and pagan literature before going on to recur in Christian and secular images.

Deer that had consumed snakes were sometimes held to make for the hills, ascending to the Mount. These are referred to in Psalm 103 – 'the high hills are a refuge for the stags' – and Psalm 17: 'He maketh my feet like hind's feet, and setteth me upon the high places.'

Sir Thomas Malory reflects popular medieval thinking when he translates a thirteenth-century passage:

> And well ought oure Lorde be signifyed to an harte. For the harte, whan he is olde, he waxith yonge agayne in his whyght skynne. Right so commyth agayne oure Lorde frome deth to lyff, for He loste erthely fleysshe, that was the dedly fleysshe whych He had takyn in the wombe of the Blyssed Virgine Mary. And for that cause appered oure Lorde as a whyghte harte without spot.

Most of these well-established attributes of the stag feature in the bestiaries of the Middle Ages and can generally be related to the concept of renewal, both through the association with antlers and also via the snake and its own renewal by changing its skin. However, there are other sources that carry the tales further into related, but often inexplicable realms. Thus, for example, the hunting manual *Les Livres du roy Modus et de la royne Ratio* (*c*. 1354–76) follows other bestiary-influenced sources in describing the stag searching under an ant heap to find the snakes, but here the snake is white, it is swallowed whole and the stag then flees to the desert, where it is rejuvenated. The ant heap is explained as representing the heap of money accumulated by man, beneath which lurks the snake of covetousness.

Other sources depict the stag as a man who refuses to acknowledge love being thrown on to the ant heap and being stung into humility. Other associations are with the miracle of the Gadarene swine in which the stag is identified with Christ driving out the Devil from man into the swine. The concept of Christ as a male stag is replaced in some texts which compare Christ expiring on the Cross to a hind. The hind is identified with the earthly part of Christ which is expiring. However, like Christ, the hind can overcome evil and arise in the morning resurrected and on high. The connection between resurrection and renewal might explain the identification of deer with Christ. Another particularly common motif in Christian sculpture dating from the ninth century is that of the centaur, identified by Virgil and, later, Dante as the Devil, armed with bow and arrow hunting a stag; in these works, the stag may also be a symbol for Christ.[15]

No doubt arising from the stag's legendary ability to neutralize snake venom, the burning of stag horns to deter snakes and the use of various parts of the stag to neutralize poisons has been recorded. Within this context there grew also the mythical value of the bezoar stone. In practice these were a variety of objects, probably often cattle gall stones (deer have no gall bladder so cannot produce gall stones) or, it has been suggested, hairballs recovered from the stomach of deer, which were often mounted in gold or silver, cherished as heirlooms and dipped into the drinks of nobles as a sovereign remedy against poison. The word 'Bezoar' is derived from Persian and the practice of using such stones may have come from the East. In any case, the stones were also considered to be created from the tears of deer. Here there is an association with the infra-orbital gland of deer, which dilates during the rut and at times of stress. This gland is a small pouch into which it is simple to insert a finger

The stag's infra-orbital gland, open and closed. According to early authorities, this gland was the seat of the bezoar stone formed from a stag's congealed tears shed after consuming serpents. The bezoar stone was highly valued as protection against poisons.

and in which there is normally a waxy exudate whose function remains unknown, although in some deer species it is used for marking territory.[16]

There is a reference to this in George Gascoigne's *Noble Arte of Venerie*:

My tears congealed to gumme, by pieces from me fall,
And thee preserve from pestilence, in pomander or ball.
Such wholesome teares shedde I, when thou pursuest
    me so.

In al-Damiri's zoological encyclopedia from the fourteenth
century we read:

> If it (the deer) is bitten by any one of them (snakes),
> tears flow from its eyes to the hollows which are under
> the sockets of its eyes, and which are deep enough to
> admit a finger. The tears get congealed and become lus-
> trous, like the sun, in which state they are used as an
> antidote for snake poison, and are known as the animal
> bazoar stone.[17]

Renaissance and humanist writers and artists developed the
emblematic value of the stag far beyond Christian motifs. Thus
we see Time's chariot often drawn by stags. Occasionally the
stags are winged and placed there as symbols of speed but the
association with Time through longevity must also be a factor.

At the same time, stags were deemed timid and cowardly.
Through punning on the words *cervus/servus* they were also
associated with servitude. Stags also became hieroglyphs for
flattery (because they are easily seduced by music), longevity and
forbidden knowledge. Many meanings were, of course, based on
classical literature. Thus the association with swiftness apparently arose because Achilles was fed on venison by Chiron, and
Telephus was brought up by a hind. Other iconologies became
even more recondite in the late sixteenth century and early
seventeenth. By this time the notion of stags renewing themselves after eating snakes was giving way to the more credible

Rosa Bonheur, *Deer in Repose*, 1867. Bonheur depicts the perfect roe deer family in this painting. Roe deer have been icons of family life since ancient times.

idea of the stag needing to drink after or during the chase, or after being struck by an arrow.

A symbolic value discrete from the above emblems relates to the antlers. This appears to have originated uniquely in *Les Livres du roy Modus et de la royne Ratio*, in which Queen Ratio identifies the ten points on the antlers with the Ten Commandments or, in the case of the cruciferous stag, with the ten fingers of the clerics dispensing the bread and wine. She also relates the crowns of the antlers to emperors and kings, seeming to suggest that male deer may symbolize all those of noble rank who sustain the faith.[18]

For us in the twenty-first century, the world of medieval and Renaissance symbolism seems esoteric and confusing. But for

George Gilbert
Scott, capital
on a column
at Glasgow
University,
1867–70.

the medieval consumer of paintings, song and poetry it was
endlessly fascinating and a way of making coded communication with like minds. Thus, for example, deer within a park are
sometimes connected by symbolism to the *hortus conclusus*, the
rose garden, and the Virgin Mary, ensuring that there was a
continuing link between deer and courtly love. And the roe deer,
which is not gregarious and is normally seen in small groups,
became an established symbol for family harmony.

As a refreshing contrast to the esoteric symbolism of the
hieroglyphers and emblematists, images of deer also recur in
a naive and purely decorative sense. Any walk through a European museum will show the use of deer to decorate objects as
diverse as English Delftware, embroidered samplers and drinking vessels. Refreshingly, their craftsmen often used images for
no clear symbolic purpose.

In India it is well recognized that the Buddha preached his
first sermon in the Deer Park at Sarnath near Benares in about

This stone was erected on the house of the keeper of the royal deer park at Falkland, Fife, in 1607. His hunting horn (*top left*) is his mark of office. As shown, the park also has a swannery. The legend ('CONTENTMENT . . .') encapsulates the notion of a park as a secluded paradise.

400 BC. This is now known as the Deer Park Sermon, and it suggests that the closed space of a game reserve, a paradise, was deliberately selected as being tranquil and perhaps imbued with spiritual connotations.

Finally a strange modern symbolism from Brazil: it is well known in that country that the Portuguese word for deer, *veados*, is used to describe gay men, apparently because Brazilians think that gay men move like deer!

6 Deer in North America

The first deer from Asia reached America across Beringia, the region of flat plains around the modern Bering Straits, about five million years ago. From the north the wapiti, members of the red deer group, went south as far as California but the white-tailed deer radiated to colonize the entire American continent from Alaska to Chile. Moose and reindeer followed much later and remained in the north.[1]

For most North Americans the white-tailed deer – and, to a lesser extent, its relatives the mule and black-tailed deer – are *the* deer. They were the quintessential prey species of the Native Americans and of enormous economic importance to the European settlers who feasted off them at the first Thanksgiving. They subsequently killed them in colossal numbers until, by the late nineteenth century, they were extinct in many areas. Populations have recovered and the deer are present now in all but five states of the USA. Unlike Old World deer species, the white-tailed deer's antlers are cast between late December and February; as in the moose, the new antler does not begin to develop until early spring.

The black-tailed deer seem to have differentiated from white-tailed in western north America around two million years ago and the mule deer, a sub-species of the black-tailed thought to be the most recent of all deer species, may have evolved from the

Victor Gifford Audubon, *Startled Deer: A Prairie Scene*, c. 1847. In the 1840s the onslaught on deer numbers was beginning in the East of America.

black-tailed only around 10,000 years ago, perhaps as much as 5,000 years after the first humans reached America.[2] As in most prehistoric cultures throughout Eurasia, in pre-Columbian North America deer had a pivotal position as the most widespread and valued quarry for humans. Locally some tribes depended on fish and shellfish and many on the buffalo. But although we think of the buffalo as the vital prey species for the Native Americans, that was only true of those people living in the Great Plains area. For the majority, especially those situated east of the Mississippi and in the north, deer were the staple. Indeed, caribou provided for all the needs of many Inuit tribes into modern times. At the misnamed Buffalo Village in West Virginia, an archaeological site at which the remains of three different Native American villages were found, the oldest dating from 4000 BC and the most recent inhabited up to 1600 AD, 44 per cent of bone remains were from deer, allowing archaeologists to state that perhaps 90 per cent of their meat came from the animal.

Deer bones provided tips for weapons, needles, fish hooks and much more, and were even made into whistles and flutes, while the hooves were used as rattles. The hard antler was used to shape stone tools and for arrow and spear tips, and when boiled it provided glue, as did the hooves. Both antler and bone was used decoratively while the hair was used in embroidery and to insulate clothing. The teeth were worn as pendants and were also used as graters to remove corn from its husk. All the meat, including offal and bone marrow, was eaten and some tribes ate the stomach contents too, while the fat was rendered into tallow and poured into the stomachs, bladder, large intestine and so on. If meat could not be eaten when fresh it was stored by drying or, after pounding and mixing with berries, preserved as pemmican. Deer were used for almost all human needs: the skins provided clothing, teepees, bedding, bags, drums, thongs and snares. Deer sinew was used for thread and bowstrings. Buckskin clothes and venison jerky were ubiquitous. Inevitably, as in Asia, and for the same reasons, North American shamanism involved deer.

Native Americans disguised in deerskins and armed with bows and arrows stealthily approaching their quarry.

When Europeans arrived in North America they met Native Americans who had experienced thousands of years of a mutually evolving and close relationship between hunter and quarry. We can even say that this had become beneficial to both men and deer, a symbiosis, a proto-domestication, since the fires started by native peoples created a more open country in which the woods became interspersed with treeless glades, benefitting the deer, whose population could then increase. Inevitably, too, there are accounts of deer being tamed. When Spanish missionaries reached Mexico, they reported entering a Mayan village that had been recently deserted. The fires were still warm, yet the only signs of life were some tame deer.

The creation myths of many Native American peoples involve deer and sometimes establish traditions demanding respect for the animal. The Navajo have a Deer Huntingway religious tradition in which successive deer are transformed as they walk in front of a concealed hunter with an arrow in his bow: first into a specific plant, such as a dead tree, and then into a person. After a large buck, an adult doe and a young buck comes a fawn. It is the fawn who, becoming a young girl, forbids the hunter from speaking badly of deer, on pain of death. She goes on to detail the ways in which slain deer must be placed on a bed of plants, of which the growing tips must point to the hunter's home. After the meat has been eaten, the bones must be placed under good plants or in other specific places with a sprinkling of yellow pollen.[3]

The same Deer Huntingway tradition decrees that nothing must be wasted from the deer, since within it is the entire environment, from the sacred mountains to plants, insects, jewels, corn, rainbows, lightning and sunlight. 'All livestock lives because of the deer. And animals are our food. They are our thoughts.' This notion of the spirit of the hunted animal entering the hunter is very common in the traditions of hunting communities – not surprisingly, since the more effectively the hunter can identify with his quarry, the better hunter he will be in his ability to anticipate every move the animal makes. The ritual treatment of the body of the animal is a way of appeasing the guilt of the hunter in having killed another animal with which he has become supernaturally close. So the modern German and central European hunter still gives the dead animal a last mouthful by placing a sprig of foliage in its mouth. Tales of the respect, indeed reverence, with which hunting peoples treated their prey are legion. Deer were referred to by the people of the Acoma Pueblo in New Mexico in a term that can be translated as 'our mother'.[4]

In the Navajo Stalking Way tradition a turquoise bead is placed between the antlers of the first deer to be killed in a hunt if it is male, or a white shell if she is female. The deer is then addressed in a prayer asking that it return to its home and that both the hunter and the deer will continue to live happily.

There was a widespread belief that deer that were killed without their hides being pierced were privileged, and the Hopi believed that they might then go 'home' to live again. Navajos learned that if they could come upon deer in open country they could eventually run them down since the white-tailed deer cannot sustain a fast pace for a long time. Once caught, the deer were placed gently on the ground and suffocated, while the hunters let them inhale pollen and sang to them. Hides procured in this fashion were especially esteemed for use in ceremonies as well as being worn as a disguise to allow the hunter to enter the company of groups of live deer.[5]

We would all like to believe that hunter-gatherer societies existed in perfect harmony with their prey species and that they evolved cultures that made overexploitation a tabu. That would seem to be the ideal to which hunter societies with the traditions we have touched on above aspire. In North America, by and large, that would seem to have been achieved. Certainly there are accounts of massive bison kills where the people were completely unable to use what they had killed, but it is never easy to disentangle those tales from the prejudices through which the Europeans observed what was happening.

It does not seem that it would be possible to overkill a population by 'still-hunting', in which a single Native American hunter moves silently through the woods to approach and kill the unsuspecting deer with his arrow. Even with the greatest skills developed over many generations, if the hunter dressed himself in a deer's skin with its antlers on his head and saw through the animal's eyeholes, we cannot imagine how very large numbers of deer could be killed. This elaborate decoy was practised to allow hunters to approach their prey very closely, not only in North America but also in Europe and Asia. The medieval hunting manual of Gaston Phébus catalogues the many decoy techniques that could be used. Calling to imitate distressed young and so attract the mother, or, during the mating season, imitating the rutting male to elicit challenges from other males, were commonplace hunting methods that are still used to this day. However, more effective – if perhaps less romantic – means of killing deer were also in use.

There are accounts of Native Americans hunting moose by driving them into water and attacking them from canoes with spears, sometimes collaboratively beating up a large tract of country to force the moose into a lake in which canoes were waiting. Sometimes the Cree would train dogs to do all the beating and driving while they waited in canoes. Deer were less difficult to manage than moose and could be more easily killed by bow and arrow or by being driven into water, where

a hind leg could be grasped and the animal's throat cut. Samuel Champlain, the French navigator who founded Quebec, described in the early seventeenth century how he saw 400–500 Huron walking abreast in line so as to drive animals into the river, where they could be more easily shot or taken from canoes.[6]

Almost universally across the globe we find that the local grazing animals have been hunted by driving them between converging fences, and then into pens in which they could be enclosed and killed. Thus Champlain in 1615 describes the Huron driving deer into a funnel about 1,500 paces long defined by fences 8 or 9 feet high. The beaters, starting before daybreak about two miles from the funnel, walked 80 yards apart,

An illustration from Gaston Phebus, *Le Livre de Chasse*, 1387–9, showing deer being tricked by a crossbowman's very unlifelike stalking horse.

An engraving of 1703 depicting Native Americans driving deer into an enclosure. Although obviously diagrammatic, this was an important way in which deer were harvested.

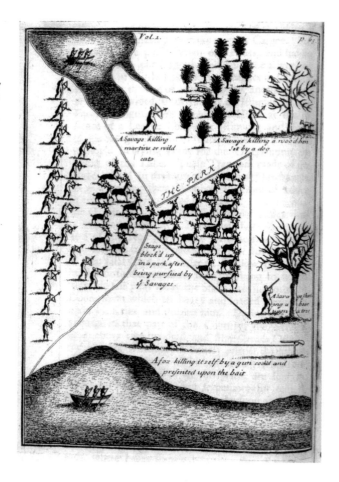

Vol.1.   p. 95

A Savage killing martins or wild cats

A Savage killing a wood hen set by a dog

THE PARK

Stags block'd up in a park, after being pursued by ye Savages.

A Savage shooting a bear upon a tree

A fox killing it self by a gun cockt and presented upon the bait

tapping two sticks together, until the deer had entered the raceway. They then imitated wolves and rushed the deer through a 5-foot gap into a small pen. Snares were laid as insurance against the pen collapsing. By repeating the drive every two days, they killed 120 deer in 38 days. Many funnel traps were

An ancient pitfall trap for reindeer in Scandinavia, a very simple and timeless system of taking and killing deer, practised wherever big game were hunted.

much longer than this one. One in upstate New York was 3 miles long and two in Wisconsin measured 12 and 15 miles.[7]

Snares were made of twisted moose hide and were commonly used by Native American people and later by white settlers. As in Russia and Norway, Native Americans used pitfall traps. A seventeenth-century Frenchman described working in Canada with native people, pursuing moose through thick snow. By using snowshoes they could overtake the moose in less than a mile in crusted snow, but in soft snow it might take 12 miles. Dogs were used to bring the moose to bay. If the snow conditions were ideal, deer could be pursued in snow crust and finally dispatched using only the tomahawk. Sometimes moose were hunted at night by 'jacking', that is to say, using burning branches to illuminate the eyes of the moose, which could then be shot by firearm or by bow.

I speculated earlier that Mesolithic people could have harvested deer and their antlers by attracting them to browse. It is gratifying to learn, then, that the Chippewa used to cut white cedar trees to attract deer, which they could then shoot with bow and arrow at night.

Fire was used by Native Americans to drive game. A late eighteenth-century witness saw 500 Iroquois encircle an area of about 50 square miles before setting fires that drove game into the centre, where a group of hunters awaited them.

Richard Nelson, a cultural anthropologist, spent several years during the late twentieth century with the Koyukon in Alaska, and consistently saw them limit their take of wild animals. With modern weapons, vehicles and tackle they could easily have harvested many more. He came away convinced that Native Americans 'understood the dangers of over-exploitation and tried to prevent it'.[8]

Inevitably, those people who migrated into America from Europe were not only of non-conformist religious persuasion but also of temperament. No doubt many had already practised illegal hunting; indeed, some were convicts who had been transported as punishment. We may imagine that something of the Robin Hood mentality travelled with many settlers. Leaving countries in which hunting was the preserve of the wealthy and landed, the early settlers suddenly found themselves in a nirvana in which the frontier appeared to belong to no-one and hunting was a lawless free-for-all.

Whatever codes the Native Americans had created for themselves and however much they observed them, they were all brought to nought by the settlers. When Europeans first made contact with the Huron, the tribe numbered about 18,000. It has been suggested they used up to 62,000 deer skins each year. Yet the European settlers universally expressed astonishment at the abundant game when they arrived and embarked on an orgy of slaughter, both themselves and through the Native Americans. They encouraged the native people to trade so that in 1716 at Charleston, South Dakota, Cherokees were paying 35 deerskins for a rifle, sixteen for a blanket, five for an axe and three for a hoe, while one skin bought 30 rounds of ammunition. Deerskin also became a currency for the settlers. In 1794 the governor of what was to become Tennessee received as his pay 1,000 deerskins, and the chief justice 500, while the residents could pay their land taxes in skins.

Between 1776 and 1850 the human population of America increased from 1.5 million to 23 million, while by the early 1800s that of the white-tailed deer had declined by 35 to 50 per cent from pre-Columbian levels. Deerskins were exported to Britain at first – 600,000 went from Savannah to England between 1755 and 1773 – but 100 years later the trade was directed to the big new cities of the eastern USA. A single Texas trader shipped 75,000 deerskins between 1844 and 1850. The skins were used for clothing, upholstery, gloves, handbags and saddles, with the hair being used for stuffing saddles and upholstery. Antler was used for buttons and knife handles, but it was also processed into ammonia and size. Venison was also being shipped: in 1880 Michigan sent 100,000 carcasses east. Venison sold for a dollar a carcass – hence the word 'buck' for dollar.[9]

Deer were killed all year round by every imaginable means: snares, pitfalls, lamping at night and hunting by men on foot or horseback, with or without dogs. It could not last. By 1832, when James Fenimore Cooper wrote an introduction to the second edition of *The Pioneers*, he commented that 'the rifle and the activity of the settlers have driven [the deer] to other haunts'.[10]

As deer numbers fell, close seasons were introduced, beginning in the east with Virginia in 1699. By 1705 the first law regulating the hunting of white-tailed deer in several counties of New York was enacted to prohibit their killing except between 1 August and 1 January. The regulation became statewide in 1788. Massachusetts, Pennsylvania and North Carolina all introduced close seasons in the early eighteenth century and states further

'"Hunting deer": a deer hunt near Deadwood in winter '87 and '88. Two miners McMillan and Hubbard got their game.' These were the final years of the massive deer culls in America. Soon close seasons were put in place and deer numbers began to rise.

west followed in the nineteenth: Texas in 1881 and Oregon in 1899. By 1890 the U.S. Bureau of Biological Survey estimated that only 300,000 white-tailed deer remained in the USA. In New York state, Pennsylvania and New Jersey, they became very rare. Deer were captured in areas of abundance and used to restock places where they were scanty or non-existent. Laws were passed making it illegal to kill deer that were not carrying antlers, so that doe numbers rose. By the mid-twentieth century there was heavy winter mortality among the deer, indicating that deer numbers had already reached too high a level in the north. In Wisconsin white-tailed deer numbers rose from 500,000 in 1950 to 1.5 million by 1995, yet the deer hunting season remained unchanged at nine days until 1996, when an additional four days of doe hunting were permitted.[11]

A new type of hunter gradually began to appear: one who took pride in killing no more than he could eat and for whom the study of wildlife and the environment became a duty. From these pioneers of a new philosophy sprang the conservation movement, which became a source of national pride, marked by the presidency of the noted hunter-turned-conservationist Theodore Roosevelt. Preserves were developed, with the first National Park at Yellowstone in 1872 and the Adirondacks in 1885, followed, of course, by many more.[12]

Heads of deer shot by hunters, Mason, Texas. Concerns about chronic wasting disease in U.S. deer require hunters to present heads for veterinary examination.

The forests changed too. As Richard Nelson points out in *Heart and Blood – Living with Deer in America*, in 1850 wood supplied 90 per cent of American fuel, but by 1970 it was only supplying 3 per cent. He goes on to explain that in 1910 more than one-third of U.S. farmland was devoted to producing feed for her 50 million horses. Yet, while pressures on some American forests have declined, that is far outweighed by the demands to clear ground for crops to feed livestock and people. In addition, commercial logging practices of clear felling, which are incompatible with the provision of browse, have further reduced available habitat for deer.

In the USA by 1900 concern for the ravaged environment had reached such a pitch that the Lacey Act was introduced, making it illegal to trade wildlife: commercial hunting finally withered away and the sale of indigenous venison became illegal.

Across the Atlantic in Europe, populations of deer, which had been virtually eliminated by the end of the eighteenth century, gradually began to recover their numbers with growing urbanization, though perhaps on a smaller scale than in the U.S. In Scotland, for example, deer numbers had reached their nadir in the late eighteenth century, coinciding with the peak in the rural human population.[13] However, with the collapse of rural populations in the famines and evictions of the nineteenth

DON'T KILL
OUR WILD LIFE

DEPARTMENT OF THE INTERIOR NATIONAL PARK SERVICE

MADE BY WORKS PROGRESS ADMINISTRATION · FEDERAL ART PROJECT NYC

Worthington Whittredge (1820–1910), *Deer, Mount Storm Park, Cincinnati*, oil on canvas. An interesting record of deer kept enclosed in 19th-century America.

century, deer began to recover, leading eventually to the demand by Scottish ecologists in the late twentieth century for drastic population reductions. In the USA the same pattern developed: overexploitation on a massive scale was eventually controlled by regulation and deer numbers began to increase once more. Deer were captured and transported to restock depleted areas and reserves. By the 1940s farmers in the state of New York were complaining of the damage caused by deer. By 1978 the deer population in the state was estimated at 450,000 and by 1993, almost one million.[14]

The hunting of deer within North America today represents a colossal mobilization of hunters and weapons, and is deeply embedded in the culture, as represented, for example, in the movies *Jeremiah Johnson* (dir. Sydney Pollack, 1972) and *Dances with Wolves* (dir. Kevin Costner, 1990). These films treat deer hunters as morally upright quasi-heroic figures and there are still very large numbers of Americans who see it as their duty to teach their sons to hunt. However, these traditional attitudes are in retreat.

A poster issued by the USA's National Park Service in response to the wave of car ownership that swept America in the 1920s and after. The concern was to increase deer numbers.

Early deer hunters such as James Fenimore Cooper's fictional Natty Bumppo in *The Pioneers* are mythologized in American culture. In 1923 D. H. Lawrence eulogized Cooper's character as seeming to 'have been born under a hemlock tree out of a pine cone . . . He is silent, simple, philosophic, moralistic and an unerring shot', inhabiting a wilderness 'lovelier than any place created in language'. This hero of American folklore craved 'no cloth better than the skin of a deer, nor any meat richer than his flesh . . . Strong it is, and strong it makes him who eats it!' He had 'never yet pulled a trigger . . . unless when food or clothes was wanting'.

Bumppo seems to have been an exception, as most hunters were killing for the market until the late nineteenth century. Meanwhile, the exploits of true-life characters such as John James Audubon, Nat Foster (on whom Bumppo was based), Meshach Browning, John Dean Caton, Theodore Van Dyke, Archibald Rutledge and many others are deeply embedded in American culture.[15]

The book *Bambi: A Life in the Woods* by Felix Salten, published in Austria in 1923, provided a story that was the inspiration for the groundbreaking and hugely influential Walt Disney animation. This film, released in 1942 at a time when many Americans were away at war, has the hunter kill Bambi's mother. It has been argued that this projects the hunter as an armed 'baddy'. Indeed the movie critic Roger Ebert has described Bambi as 'a parable of sexism, nihilism and despair, portraying absentee fathers and passive mothers in a world of violence'.[16]

Felix Salten had written a much more realistic story set in a natural environment. It includes a vigorous rut and deer dying of winter starvation. Certainly the deer can speak, and the book is undeniably for children, but it pulls no punches. There is an accurate and delightful description of the summer warmth in the meadow, and also of the cold, long winters while Bambi grows up steadily into an adult stag. But his mother's death is no severe trauma and takes place only when Bambi is able to be independent. Nor is he ever alone but is supported by his beloved Faline, for whom he fights other stags. 'He', the vicious man who kills Bambi's mother during the pheasant drive, is to some extent redeemed by taking the wounded Gobo in and feeding him until spring when he returns to the forest, albeit having lost all his knowing cervine woodcraft, to be welcomed by his mother and sister.

By contrast, in the film, Disney deliberately sentimentalizes and simplifies the tale, anthropomorphizing the deer by making their eyes huge with long lashes, shortening their noses, rounding their heads and making them move and act like humans. This was part of a highly successful plan to engage the viewers' emotions. He has Bambi's mother brutally killed and Bambi orphaned. Bambi attempts to rescue Faline from the hounds and is wounded by a bullet, while the hunters start a fire that devastates the woodland. Admittedly there is an epilogue in which Bambi stares fondly at Faline and her newborn twins, but this vision of rebirth is not the memory children will take away from the film. The anthropologist Matt Cartmill has described Bambi as 'probably the most effective piece of antihunting propoganda ever made'. It depicts man as irredeemably wicked in a simplistic travesty of the complex ecology of the forest of which He, man, is a part. The 'Bambi factor' continues to haunt those who are trying to manage wildlife in a rational objective way for the good of the environment.[17]

Books such as *The Yearling* (1938) by Marjorie Kinnan Rawlings and *People of the Deer* (1952) by Farley Mowat helped to secure a different place for deer within the modern American psyche in the mid-twentieth century. But perhaps even more influential, and reinforcing the Bambi image, was the story of *Rudolph, the Red-Nosed Reindeer*.

The origin of the Santa Claus myth, although far removed from Rudolph, lies, it is often said, with the Saami reindeer herders in northern Scandinavia. They are reputed to have fed their reindeer on fly agaric fungi. This contains psychedelic compounds that cause the reindeer to leap about. The reindeer herders then collect and drink the urine from their deer, because they have by then metabolised most of the toxins. The resulting drink gives the Saami a high, so perhaps it is in their minds that the reindeer are flying.[18] While it had a longstanding history in Europe, the Santa Claus myth really took hold in North America with the publication in 1823 of the anonymous poem 'A Visit from Saint Nicholas', which introduced the idea of Santa Claus living at the North Pole with elves and eight named flying reindeer that would pull his sleighload of presents to be delivered to children at Christmas. The political cartoonist Thomas Nast then developed the notion of the red-coated bearded character in the late nineteenth century with ideas that were further taken up by L. Frank Baum in 1902 in his *The Life and Adventure of Santa Claus*. The notion of the ninth reindeer, Rudolph, with his red nose, was introduced in a 1939 booklet by Robert May, followed by Gene Autry's song in 1949.

As the North American population has become steadily more urbanized and has been inevitably influenced by *Bambi* and *Rudolph*, there has been a progressively more negative approach to hunting. In the film *The Deer Hunter* (dir. Michael Cimino, 1978) the hunters are arguably vilified to some extent: hunting is the trigger for guilty and stressful flashbacks of experiences in the Vietnam war. This reflects the view that hunting is now no longer morally unquestioned and opinions have become polarized. Deer are no longer a staple American food resource

– indeed, since 1900 the sale of indigenous venison has been a felony – and the image of deer has changed. Robert Wegner cites the pro-hunting advocate James Swan as describing positive, pleasurable motives in the mind of the hunter, and ones that 'cultivate respect for nature that is the root of the true conservationist'.[19] Yet these are becoming more confused:

> Deer hunters are currently an endangered minority fast fading into the dustbins of history. We now constitute less than nine percent of the population and our actual numbers continue to shrink. With increasing deer numbers nationwide and decreasing hunter numbers, we are reaching the upper limits of deer management via deer hunting. Worse, the paradigm of managing a public resource on private property is broke.[20]

By the end of the twentieth century, ecologists were worried about damage to the habitat, gardeners and farmers and foresters were concerned about their crops and increasing numbers of people were being killed and injured in road traffic accidents caused by deer. Deer themselves were being killed too, of course. Nelson cites figures for Wisconsin, where 400 deer were killed by cars in 1961, with the death toll reaching between 35,000 and 50,000, 30 years later. The accidents injured 800 people per year and led to insurance claims of $100 million per annum in the state. In addition, the state spends $200,000 each year collecting the dead deer. Attempts to reduce deer and car collisions by installing reflectors to warn the deer away can be effective but cost $7,500 per mile on two-lane roads and twice as much on four-lane highways in Boulder, Colorado, where cars can kill 16 to 19 per cent of the deer population in one year. And it's not just cars: by 1991 eight deer had been hit by aircraft at Dulles International Airport outside Washington, DC.[21] Figures for the USA overall show that each year about 150 people and 1.5 million deer are killed in collisions between deer and automobiles, at a total cost of over $1 billion. Inevitably, even more deer are injured in an unknown depth of suffering.

Not only do deer kill people on the roads, but they have an unfortunate association with Lyme disease. Although deer do not themselves carry the causative agent of Lyme disease, the bacteria *Borrelia burgdorferi* and its relatives, they do provide blood meals for the ticks that transmit the disease. They are therefore apparently irreversibly associated with Lyme disease in the public eye, partly because of the fact that the tick involved has been popularly known in the USA as the deer tick for many years. Deer are the villains of the piece.

Where protection is in place, deer numbers sometimes grow to such an extent that habitat is damaged and winter deer mortality becomes unacceptably high. With many people reluctant to countenance the hunting or culling of deer especially in reserves, and with the decline of hunters wanting to shoot deer, their populations continue to grow and the animals extend their range into suburbia. The illegality of selling the venison arguably exacerbates the situation. There seems no answer to these problems that will content all parties. Nelson points out that while in rural areas culling the deer would not be controversial, 'the urban view . . . is predominantly aesthetic rather than utilitarian'. Yet perhaps we underestimate people's understanding. A study by Michael Satchell and Joannie Schrof cited by Nelson found that more than 80 per cent of Americans approve of hunting 'to put game on the table' while 80 per cent disapproved of hunting for trophies to hang on the wall and 60 per cent of hunting for sport. This is a common viewpoint. There is popular abhorrence of 'killing for pleasure'.[22] This too is simplistic, of course, for the subsistence hunter would not survive long if he did not enjoy hunting: no hunter is effective if he does not find pleasure in the chase, in becoming one with nature. At some point education, coupled with economic necessity, may change public attitudes, and a growing realization that hunting is necessary to prevent over-population and resultant habitat degradation, and to create a healthy deer population, may dawn.

In the Netherlands a trial has been established against the background of an urban population that generally opposes hunting. In a large reclaimed polder called the Oostvaarder-splassen red deer, cattle, and horses were introduced with the intention of leaving them to fend for themselves. The principal object of the trial was to assess changes to the vegetation but when large numbers of the animals began after some years to starve to death each winter the experiment exposed interesting public attitudes. It appeared that a majority of Dutch citizens preferred to allow the animals to starve rather than allow hunters to intervene. It was agreed that the animals should only be shot when they reached the point where they could no longer stand up and walk. The experiment continues.[23]

What are the alternatives to controlling deer by shooting them? Catching deer and removing them to less populated areas is stressful for the deer. Many animals are likely to die during the procedure or after relocation: Nelson gives figures of 83 per cent of relocated deer dying within one year in one case, and other studies show between 25 and 68 per cent. Areas that can justify this procedure have been described as 'rich enough to make their deer die somewhere else'. Catching deer and administering drugs to render them sterile is also stressful, and catching a worthwhile percentage is usually impossible. In addition, the chemicals used will normally require repeated treatments. Feeding deer drugs to render them sterile is potentially polluting in distributing biologically active chemicals within the environment. Both these procedures are very expensive and the sight of a population of ageing and infirm sterile deer may disturb some people too. The introduction of predators upsets some animal rights groups but is at least the most natural solution; whether it is effective is still not clear, and the predators may kill livestock and even occasionally people. In any case, cougars or mountain lions, for example, are bound to increase by themselves and are now becoming more common in some suburban areas.

Having said all that, some suburban and urban communities seem willing to accept the problems associated with deer in their gardens and on their roads, fencing them out where they are finding damage intolerable. Nelson cites Boulder, Colorado, as reaching this degree of co-habitation but points out that cougars are now moving in after the deer and preying on dogs and cats.

Modern writers seriously concerned with deer and the environment generally accept that human hunters are the most humane solution to deer overpopulation. They express concern that the number of hunters is declining and many take the stance that hunting is a deeply time-honoured occupation that is spiritually improving and refreshes the bond between humans and the environment. It could be that the suburban deer problem might be a route to educating the human inhabitants.

Throughout the USA there are an estimated twelve million deer hunters and while most of those use private land, a few pay for the privilege of hunting on trophy ranches. They benefit the economy by $700 million directly in payment for hunting licenses, but hunting-related trade overall is thought to generate $11.8 billion per annum.[24]

In his essay 'Wildlife in American Culture' the great American ecologist and environmentalist Aldo Leopold asks deer-hunters to 're-enact their cultural past, create cultural values from our deer hunting heritage, be aware of them and create a pattern for their continued growth'. It is unclear whether that is the spiritual experience of those hunting on ranches, where deer are fed and protected until they grow to be significant trophies.

Hunters in Texas kill between 350,000 and 555,000 of the state's 3.5 million white-tailed deer each year, and only a small proportion of those are shot on hunting ranches. In any case, for all hunters, the primeval experience of sitting quietly in the dusk watching wildlife is preserved and must be beneficial in a society where silence is rare. Much less than half of those hunters with licenses will kill a deer, yet sociological research has shown that they value the opportunity to wander quietly through the woods, always anticipating the excitement of direct contact with nature.

Texas may be the state with the most white-tailed deer but it is also the one with the most exotic species. Leaving aside the antelope, Texas has large populations of Eurasian deer, principally fallow, axis and sika. There is concern that these species can outperform the native deer and since they are 'exotics' their venison can legally be sold, which some fear might open the door to the illegal sales of meat from indigenous species. In fact, most venison retailed in the USA is probably imported from New Zealand and there is as yet no sign of deer being overhunted.

In the USA as in other developed countries, hunter numbers are in decline as deer numbers are increasing, although women hunters are playing an increasing role.

7 Deer and People Today

There is a cyclical pattern common to most, perhaps all, deer populations in developed countries. Historically, as the human rural population has grown, deer numbers have declined. People are presumably responsible for this by killing and eating the deer. It is not easy to tell for sure, because in most historical situations this was illicit. In England we find many records of poaching in the forest courts during the medieval period. Jean Birrell has examined some of these accounts, which provide a remarkable and fascinating picture of the peasant killing the deer by skilled woodcraft using snares plaited from horsehair, sharpened wooden stakes and so on. The more conventional bow and arrow were not favoured, as wounded deer carrying an arrow would draw attention to the crime.[1] Although descriptions of such poaching are common in the surviving records, they can only be the very tip of a large iceberg. Medieval coppiced woodland and small parcels of cropping must have made up a large part of the countryside, and this would have been an ideal habitat for deer.

Now, even with modern rifles, we find it hard to control deer numbers throughout Europe, which gives us an idea of just how widespread must have been the poaching in order to lead to a decline in deer numbers. When the Normans arrived in England they greatly strengthened the measures taken by the Saxon rulers to restrict hunting and created forests and forest laws. These may not have been enforced to their brutal fullest extent but nevertheless make clear that there was concern to protect the deer. By the sixteenth century deer had been eliminated from many areas and by the end of the eighteenth century it is no exaggeration to say that they were on the verge of extinction; indeed, roe deer may actually have been extinct.

But then, the movement of people into the cities that had always gone on gathered pace, and the human rural population began to decline. Outliers that had escaped the cart and the hounds, and escapees from shrinking deer parks, often formed the basis of new populations. By the middle of the twentieth century, deer numbers were increasing. Roe were reintroduced and deer were protected for the new sport of stalking.[2]

In the Scottish Highlands red deer had survived the dramatic growth in the human population of the eighteenth century, albeit in much reduced numbers. With the sudden decline of the rural population caused by the evictions that we know as the Clearances, the glens were almost deserted, and became the sporting estates of the Victorians. For more than two centuries the deer in them enjoyed protection as the sporting lairds conserved them, but they never quite shot enough, and from 150,000 in 1965, Scottish red deer numbers had reached some 300,000 by 1995. Then came concerns from environmentalists that the deer were preventing regeneration and reducing biodiversity. Many of the sporting landowners were replaced by new landlords eager to reduce deer populations, such as the National Trust, the Royal Society for the Protection of Birds and the John Muir Trust, and in the early years of this century deer numbers have fallen again.

The Isle of Rum off the west coast of Scotland provides an interesting microcosm of the population dynamics of the two species: human and deer. It is not clear when or how red deer reached Rum after the last glaciation. It seems unlikely that they could have swum. Perhaps they were introduced from the mainland by Neolithic or even Mesolithic settlers. Certainly there are signs of Mesolithic settlement. In 1549 Monro, Dean of the Isles, describes an 'abundance of little deir' and birds with 'few to start them except deire'. By 1703 Martin Martin could record that 'the mountains have some hundred of deer grazing in them'. He goes on to describe how the chief of clan Maclean supported a tabu on the killing of deer on the mountain of Fionchra, perhaps a measure that had evolved to maintain the deer population. However, it proved ineffective, because when Thomas Pennant visited the island in 1771 he stated that there were only 80 deer. James Boswell in 1786 and Walker in 1808 mention that there were still thought to be deer on Rum, but by 1796 the Old Statistical Account noted that 'while the wood throve the deer throve', indicating that as the human population had reached such a level as to destroy all the trees, they had also killed the last deer. In fact the human population seems to have reached a peak of about 500 around 1800, when famine was only staved off by grain shipments provided by the chief, Maclean of Coll. The island was finally depopulated to Nova Scotia in 1828 to give way for sheep, which proved uneconomic, so that by 1845 it had become a sporting estate restocked with deer. With few to kill them, the deer numbers soon reached over 1,000. This is a pattern seen in most developed countries: deer numbers and woodlands decline as the human rural population grows. When the human population peaks, the deer disappear and the woodland shrinks to its lowest levels: the human population then emigrates or moves into cities, and the deer numbers begin to rise to unprecedented levels: there is an inverse correlation between the two species.[3]

Deer are now accepted as desirable in many parts of the world as a species that, if effectively managed, can control vegetation and increase biodiversity. Deer parks are recognized as biological enclaves, which, in Britain, often contain ecologically invaluable veteran trees. In fact it has been suggested that it is because of Britain's rich heritage of deer parks that we possess more veteran trees than any other European country.[4] But those benefits are often outweighed by the damage deer cause. The concept of a cultural carrying capacity has evolved. This implies that each area of ground will have an optimum number of deer that it can sustain per acre or hectare, depending on the habitat and the needs of the local human population. Where deer numbers are too high, farm crops and especially trees suffer. Seedlings may be grazed, preventing regeneration of the forest, and older trees may be barked. Some songbirds, such as nightingales, may lose the scrub they require in which to nest, and plants such as oxlips, cowslips, orchids and bluebells may be reduced. Where the deer exist next to towns and cities, collisions with cars become a problem, and people may be worried that the deer are increasing the number of ticks, with all the concerns of tickborne diseases such as Lyme disease. Yet at the same time, the deer may be valued as visually stimulating and may maintain a popular parkland environment.

Throughout the developed world there are different laws controlling the hunting of deer. Within Europe, countries are divided between those in which the deer are *res nullius*, or belong to no-one, as in Britain, and can be shot only by the owner of the land on which they happen to be or his contracted agent; and other countries in which the deer are *res communis*, belonging to everyone, so may be shot on other people's property, but under licences issued by the community. It is more complicated than that, since in France, for example, the right to hunt rests with the landowner, but the state controls what number and category of deer may be shot.[5] Where the deer are held to be *res communis*, as in France and Spain, those who wish to avoid having hunters wander through their property can elect to do so, which explains the *Chasse Privé* or equivalent signs one sees in most European countries.

In both situations effective control of the deer depends on having a large body of motivated hunters. Norway has a higher proportion of its population registered as hunters than any other European country, at 5 per cent. In other member states the figure is around 1 per cent. In Britain around half of the deer shot are killed by 'recreational' hunters who make up 85 per cent of those stalking deer. As one would expect, professional hunters kill more deer than hobbyists. The major international problem in developed countries is that the number of hunters is declining. The human population is ageing and the often ill-informed public, increasingly urban in attitude, dislike the idea of killing deer, so there is therefore implicit disapproval of hunters. Meanwhile the habitat for deer is increasing. A total of 12 per cent of the United Kingdom is forested, a figure twice that of 1924.

In North America deer are the object of annual hunting forays that compare with the firepower of the Second World War, yet sale of the venison is a felony and increasing deer numbers create problems. The picture is very different in New Zealand, which had no mammals when first settled by Europeans. Deer released there in the nineteenth century thrived. As they destroyed the environment they were shot, and later captured live, from helicopters to form the basis of a deer-farming industry which now kills 500,000 deer per annum, principally for sale in Europe. Those farms earn £150 million per annum for the New Zealand economy. Within 40 years, a new domestic livestock species has been created.[6]

The velvet antler production for the Chinese medicine market is an important part of New Zealand deer farming, with the growing antlers of adult stags removed under local anaesthetic with veterinary supervision of trained operators. The sales of antler however, only represent about 10 per cent of the deer farmers' income, much less than the income from the hides and other by-products. The most recent available figures from New Zealand show annual export sales of farmed venison of 15,000 tonnes worth £145 million, of velvet antler £14.8 million, and of other by-products £20 million. More than 80 per cent of these sales are to Europe.[7] In New Zealand research into the possible pharmacological value of antler continues, while deer farming for venison is growing in Britain, Europe and North America. Within Europe it is illegal to remove growing antlers from live deer on humanitarian grounds. It seems inevitable that deer farming will develop within Europe as agricultural subsidies are 'decoupled', so that those farming deer will eventually receive the same encouragement as those farming the fattier red meats.

Chasse Privé signs can be seen along rural roads in France and Spain. They indicate where a landowner wishes to preserve the hunting for himself.

The trigger for New Zealand deer farming was arguably the removal of agricultural subsidies in 1987. This placed deer farming on a 'level playing field' with other pastoral livestock, notably sheep. In other countries, particularly Scotland, where deer farming began at the same time as in New Zealand, subsidies were retained for conventional livestock, placing deer at a substantial disadvantage.[8] It has not been easy for New Zealand, which has been faced with currency fluctuations and consumers who, especially in its most important market, Germany, ostensibly prefer wild venison. Now, however, all game dealers have learned that the farmed product is superior to the wild in being younger, more hygienically prepared, not suffering from bullet damage, and consistent in age and carcass size. Currently the chief problem for deer farmers in New Zealand is the very high demand for milk solids in China. This has forced the price of dairy land so high that deer farmers cannot compete, and there has been a gradual decline in production of farmed venison. This is in the face of growing demand in many parts of Europe, especially in Britain, where a populace that was effectively new to venison was suddenly exposed to farmed venison in supermarkets, farmers' markets and farm shops together with a welter of advice on how to cook it and information that explained how much healthier venison was than the fattier red meats. Venison has less fat than skinned chicken, and is very high in iron, an element in which most women in developed countries are deficient.[9]

Britain now imports about 50,000 deer carcasses from New Zealand each year, so that most venison in UK supermarkets is from New Zealand. Retailers report sales growing at 25 per cent per annum.

It seems clear that cattle and sheep as well as pigs were selected over centuries by breeders who wanted their livestock to be fat

The Chinese demand for velvet antler was a factor in the early growth of New Zealand deer farming but plays a small part now. Most of New Zealand's 1.5 million farmed deer exist to supply European markets with venison.

at a time when that fat was valuable. Now we are less active and live in heated houses, fat has become a menace, so the leaner meat of wild animals is preferable. In addition, the very long period of time during which humans ate wild animals seems to have adapted us to those meats. In contrast we have only been eating the fatty meats of domestic animals for a relatively short time and have still to adapt our metabolism to cope with this novel intake of fatty meat. We are physiologically adapted to game meat, which explains why many health authorities have recommended venison over other red meats.[10]

Even if deer farming in New Zealand is currently declining, this is unlikely to be permanent: deer farming is now there to stay. New Zealand has 3,000 deer farmers in a country with a human population less than that of Scotland. Deer are treated exactly like other pastoral livestock: weaned, ear tagged, weighed, treated for worms and sent off to abattoirs and so on. The animals are almost entirely red deer but are often mated to wapiti-cross red deer stags. Genetic improvement and artificial insemination are commonplace, with occasional embryo transfer of high-value deer.

The story of New Zealand deer farming is an extraordinary testimony to entrepreneurial flair. They have created the first new livestock species for 5,000 years, they have evolved sophisticated methods of farming deer and now they are supplying the Western world with a much healthier meat.

Not only do we manage deer on a practical level differently from our ancestors, but we also portray them in different ways, such as on film. Although now more people live in urban than rural environments, the use of deer in that most urban of media, film, still uses some of the same symbols that were attached to these animals in medieval art. Thus the concept of deer as wild, mysterious and otherworldly makes them increasingly popular in the horror-movie genre. Deer are not specific in this role: the Danish film-maker Lars von Trier used deer, but also foxes and crows, to add to the sense of evil and confusion in his acclaimed film *Antichrist* (2009), sometimes classed as an art-house horror film. In a forest dominated by Satanic activity, the human hero is deeply impressed by a fallow doe that looks at him and shows no fear. When she turns, she is seen to have a dead stillborn fawn still attached to her vulva. The foxes and crows play equally important roles. In *House of Wax* (2005) a pile of pieces of dead deer creates a similar effect.[11]

Perhaps the most significant use of deer in a recent film was as the crux of the British film *The Queen* (dir. Stephen Frears, 2006). The parallels with medieval legend are striking. During the royal family's summer stay at Balmoral for the deerstalking season, the death of Princess Diana occurs. After some agonizing, the royal family decides to conceal their feelings and assume an air of dignified grief, remaining in Scotland despite the blandishments of the Prime Minister, Tony Blair, played by Michael Sheen. Shortly afterwards the Queen, played by Helen Mirren, is driving alone in a Land Rover that breaks down while fording a Highland burn. As she awaits assistance, her mask of courageous reserve slips and she weeps. At that moment she looks up to see a wild Highland stag, actually one belonging to the author of this book, standing nearby. For a crucial moment they make eye contact and the Queen decides to present a more human face to the population by returning to London. In a subsequent scene this exceptionally large stag is shot on a neighbouring estate and the Queen travels to see the body, as if paying homage to a divine messenger. The inference is that this mysterious stag from the other world of wild things has through fate or intervention caused the Queen to reconsider her decision. This epiphany might have come straight from the distant past. In a

medieval context, the Queen out hunting, riding a horse instead of a Land Rover, would have been confronted by a stag carrying a crucifix between its antlers, which she would have felt obliged to follow. In both the ancient and modern meetings the key is in the moment of eye contact.

Deer feature with impressive frequency in other films. Usually these appearances can be classified into several types. Swash-buckling movies involving historical heroes such as Robin Hood or Robert the Bruce frequently include deer-hunting sequences. A particularly elaborate such hunt is presented in *The Three Musketeers* (dir. Richard Lester, 1973), in which captive deer are chased to their doom down a canvas-lined raceway very similar to that depicted in the Spanish painting by Juan Bautista

Juan Bautista Martínez del Mazo, *Stag Hunting at Aranjuez*, 1643, oil on canvas. In Spain, fallow deer were chased down canvas-lined raceways to be dispatched by swordsmen.

Martínez del Mazo, *Stag Hunting at Aranjuez*, now in the Prado in Madrid, which illustrates a popular entertainment pursued at the court of Philip IV in the grounds of the royal palace at Aranjuez. Christopher Lambert and Sean Connery chased one of my stags in *Highlander* (dir. Russell Mulcahy, 1986). Examples abound of screenwriters exploiting the convenient device of a car crashing into deer with any number of consequences, including a heroine cradling the dying deer in her arms, as for example, did Emma Thomson one of our calves in the television film *Blueboy* (1994); or swerving to avoid one of our stags in *Summer Solstice* (2005), an adaptation of a story by Rosamund Pilcher. These devices are effective in suddenly introducing an unpredictable 'wild' element into a comfortable controlled situation. Another much used device is that of a group of male friends, usually American, coming together on a deer hunt. This provides an opportunity for bonding, as most famously in *The Deer Hunter* (1978), in which the friends go hunting just prior to departing for Vietnam, where experiences are to test those friendships to destruction. Perhaps the hunting excursion is more commonly used to provide a dramatic sense of isolation in a remote cabin in the woods and mountains that may be especially challenging for an urban audience.

There is a more imaginative use of deer in the action thriller film *Hanna* (dir. Joe Wright, 2011). The eponymous heroine shoots a reindeer in her native Finland as a young girl, while being trained by her father to become an assassin. Later, as the denouement approaches, another deer directs her to her target. This might be construed as an example of deer symbolizing rebirth and regeneration.

In a further category of devices, deer feature as divine or supernatural beings, exploiting the mystery of these wild animals. Thus in the animated Japanese film *Princess Mononoke* (dir. Hayao Miyazaki, 1997) the heroine travels in a search for a 'deergod' to resolve her problems, and in the American television film *Deer Woman* (2005) deer change into women with references to Native American traditions. In *The Surface of Impenetrable Things* (dir. Lucy Campbell and Tigerish Walters, 2011), calculated monotony is broken by a strange otherworldly boy wearing antlers.

Other films have sought to exploit the controversial action of killing deer, and several films have used the dramatic device, as in the legend of Actaeon, of having the hunters hunted either by other humans or by some supernatural force.

In the Italian movie *La Solutudine dei Numeri Primi* (dir. Saverio Costanzo, 2010) a dream sequence features a walk down a corridor lined with the heads of deer hung on the walls as trophies. The theme of silent reproach of the hunting of deer and most especially of hanging the trophy heads on the wall has recently extended well beyond the world of film. Faux trophies of stylized antlered deer heads made of newspapers, cloth or wood grace interior design stores all over the world now, gently mocking deer hunters. In the same context there is also a vogue for artists to use the form of antlers to inspire sculpture.

Antlers have been used to construct furniture and chandeliers for centuries, reaching a particular zenith of popularity during the mid-nineteenth century in Central Europe. Several companies have now resumed production of antler furniture and it is once more fashionable. Even taxidermy is enjoying a vogue.

As a simple symbol of wild purity, with a touch of the enigmatic, and regardless of the more complex association with rebirth and renewal, deer remain strong favourites in branding. Names such as Deer Park for an American bottled water, or Haunch of Venison for a London modern art gallery, remain sound commercial choices while the deer as a decorative motif

Antler chair with tartan covering. In the 19th century antler furniture became an industry, especially in Germany. It is undergoing a revival now, in Scotland in particular.

in clothing and as a symbol of Western Christmas goes from strength to strength. Deer remain one of the most used and abused motifs in Christmas cards, reflecting the Santa Claus and/or Rudolph theme.

The use of deer for advertising extends into television commercials too. These short films are well resourced and directors can indulge themselves in very high-quality effects. We have used our deer, usually stags, for commercials promoting Land Rovers in Japan that entailed a large film crew for a week. Filmed during the rut in the autumn, a group of antlered stags had to approach the parked Land Rover through thick mist created by a smoke machine, lie down and then one by one stand up and walk away. Who ever wrote that screenplay can have had no notion of the practical difficulties involved, but we managed it on the last available half-day. Now, filming is more likely to take place against a stable background to allow computers to isolate the image and insert it into a different background post-production, which has made things easier. Thus a commercial for Glenfiddich whisky has one of my stags walking proudly down a street in Havana. Yet for lower-budget work it may still be more economical to use the live animal, so that recently we placed a stag in a Highland glen and had a model hang his smart countrywear hat on its antlers. Most advertisements in the printed media exploit American deer in what

Qi Xing, *As if James Macpherson had ever played fiddle for a white stag*, 2009. The juxtaposition of an American deer in a Scottish legend seems commonplace for this Chinese artist.

purports to be a European context. For those of us familiar with deer that seems a laughably crass error – there is scientifically as much difference between the American white-tailed deer and the Scottish red deer as between a cow and a sheep.

If the deer motif lives on in film, so do the flesh and blood animals, with a lot more controversy. In America and increasingly in Europe, as human urbanization and commuting become the norm, deer numbers grow and the image of deer as rare and precious mystical creatures risks being gradually displaced by perceptions of deer as suburban nuisances eating garden plants, spreading disease and causing road traffic accidents.

In the developed world the cycle seems complete. After near extinction in Europe in the late eighteenth century and in North America in the late nighteenth, deer are back with a vengeance. In our increasingly urban societies people see deer more and more frequently. Yet if historically the human view of deer seems to us to have been clouded with extraordinary symbolism, myth and unreality, now perhaps, cocooned in houses and cars, we understand these animals even less. From the prized and elevated icon of the hunt, deer are in danger of becoming degraded and commonplace. By an understanding of the way the different species live, and through a knowledge of their historical place in our cultures, perhaps we can help them to escape that fate and let them continue to command our respect.

Timeline of the Deer

c. 8.5 MYA	*c.* 5.5 MYA	*c.* 2 MYA	*c.* 0.5 MYA
The deer family originates	Deer cross the Bering Straits into America	The 40 species of deer differentiate	Hominins use antler to shape flints at Boxgrove in Surrey, England

c. 70 AD	100 AD	700 AD	1000 TO 1400
The placing of collars on deer described by Pliny	Romans introduce fallow deer to Fishbourne Palace, England	Legend of St Eustace first described by St John of Damascus	Some 3,000 medieval deer parks in England

1851	1854	1865	1880
Landseer paints the *Monarch of the Glen*	First red deer exported to New Zealand	Père David deer discovered by Père Armand David in Beijing	The slang term 'buck' coined as deer carcases are sold for a dollar each in Michigan

| 30,000 YEARS AGO | 3,000 TO 2,000 BC | 2,000 BC | 650 BC | 200 BC |

Deer are represented in the French Chauvet cave

Antler used to mine flints at Grimes Graves, Norfolk

Deer are represented in Mongolian pre-Bronze Age petroglyphs

Assyrian deer hunts depicted

Chinese Han dynasty scrolls explain the medicinal value of antler velvet

| 1100 | 1250 TO 1400 | 1750 | 1788 |

Normans introduce fallow deer from Sicily to Britain

Royal Warrant of venison instigated between the Ling and the citizens of London

Roe deer probably extinct in England and Wales

Close season legislation introduced to protect deer throughout New York state

| 1919 | 1970 | 1997 | 2007 |

Last British red deer released in New Zealand

Deer farming begins in New Zealand and Scotland

English National Trust 'bans' stag hunting with hounds on its properties

New Zealand annually exports over 20,000 tonnes of farmed venison

References

1 THE FAMILY OF DEER

The classification of deer is a fast-moving field and some elements remain controversial despite the valuable new results of DNA analysis. I have chosen to use the phylogeny of the Cervidae published by Clemént Gilbert, Anne Ropiquet and Alexandre Hassanin in 'Mitochon - drial and Nuclear Phylogenies of Cervidae (Mammalia, Ruminantia): Systematics, Morphology and Biogeography', *Molecular Phylogenetics and Evolution*, XL (2006), pp. 101–17. I have taken further details of the classification of the Old World deer from Christian Pitra, Joerns Fickel, Erik Meijaard and P. Colin Groves, 'Evolution and Phylogeny of Old World Deer', *Molecular Phylogenetics and Evolution*, XXXIII (2004), pp. 880–95. I have used Valerius Geist's monumental *Deer of the World: Their Evolution, Behavior and Ecology* (Shrewsbury, 1999), which provides an invaluable insight into the relationship between the behaviour and morphology of the members of the deer family and their environment. The late Kenneth Whitehead's *Deer of the World* (London, 1972) is a very useful and accessible description of the deer and especially their geographical range.

1 In categorically stating 40 species of deer, Gilbert follows P. Grubb, 'Order Artiodactyla', in *Mammal Species of the World: A Taxonomic and Geographic Reference*, ed. Don E. Wilson and DeeAnn M. Reeder, 2nd edn (Washington, DC, and London, 1993), pp. 384–92.
2 For information on the life of Sir Victor Brooke, I have used his biography by Oscar Leslie Stephen, *Sir Victor Brooke, Sportsman*

and Naturalist: A Memoir of his Life and Extracts from his Letters and Journals [*c.* 1891] (Milton Keynes, undated facsimile).

3 Pitra et al., 'Evolution and Phylogeny of Old World Deer'.

4 Geist, *Deer of the World.*

5 Gilbert et al., 'Mitochondrial and Nuclear Phylogenies of Cervidae (Mammalia, Ruminantia)', pp. 101–17.

6 Pitra et al., 'Evolution and Phylogeny of Old World Deer'.

7 Geist, *Deer of the World.*

8 Marco Masseti, 'Holocene and Anthropochorous Wild Mammals of the Mediterranean Islands', *Anthropozoologica*, XXVIII (1998), pp. 3–20; Masseti, ed., *Island of Deer: Natural history of the Fallow Deer of Rhodes and of the Vertebrates of Dodecanese, Greece* (Rhodes, 2002); Masseti, Elena Pecchioli and Cristiano Vernesi, 'Phylogeography of the Last Surviving Populations of Rhodian and Anatolian Fallow Deer (*Dama dama dama L.*, 1758)', *Biological Journal of the Linnean Society*, XCIII (2008), pp. 835–44.

9 Naomi J. Sykes, Judith White, Tina E. Hayes and Martin R. Palmer, 'Tracking Animals Using Strontium Isotopes in Teeth: The Role of Fallow Deer (*Dama dama*) in Roman Britain', *Antiquity*, LXX (2006), pp. 948–59.

10 John Fletcher, *Gardens of Earthly Delight: The History of Deer Parks* (Oxford, 2011).

11 Donald and Norma Chapman, *Fallow Deer* (Lavenham, 1975).

12 A. M. Lister, C. J.Edwards, D.A.W. Nock, M. Bruce, I. A. van Pijlen, D. G. Bradley, M. G. Thomas and I. Barnes, 'The Phylogenetic Position of the "Giant Deer" *Megaloceros giganteus*', *Nature*, CDXXXVIII (2005), pp. 850–53.

13 Pitra et al., 'Evolution and Phylogeny of Old World Deer'.

14 Geist, *Deer of the World*.

15 Ibid.

16 Ibid.

17 Gilbert et al., 'Mitochondrial and Nuclear Phylogenies of Cervidae (Mammalia, Ruminantia)'.

1 Michael Pitts and Mark Roberts, *Fairweather Eden: Life in Britain Half a Million Years Ago as Revealed by the Excavations at Boxgrove* (London, 1998).

2 There is a substantial literature on these aspects of deer biology, for example, T. H. Clutton-Brock and S. D. Albon, *Red Deer in the Highlands* (London, 1989); John Fletcher, *Fletcher's Game: A Vet's Life with Scotland's Deer* (Edinburgh, 2003); K. L. Blaxter, R.N.B. Kay, G.A.M. Sharman, J.M.M. Cunningham and W. J. Hamilton, *Farming the Red Deer: The First Report of an Investigation by the Rowett Research Institute and the Hill Farming Research Organisation* (Edinburgh, 1974).

3 Valerius Geist, *Deer of the World: Their Evolution, Behaviour and Ecology* (Shrewsbury, 1999).

4 N. G. Chapman and S. Harris, *Muntjac* (Fordingbridge and London, 1996).

5 Z. Yu, 'Development of the Chinese Deer Farming Industry and the Market for Deer Velvet', in *Advances in Antler Science and Product Technology*, 2nd International Symposium (Auckland, 2004), pp. 233–8. Much information on the velvet industry is also available from the Deer Industry New Zealand website: www.deernz.org, accessed 27 July 2012.

6 G.H.D. Darwall and R. G.Clark, 'On the Growth and Form of Deer Antlers', *Deer*, VI (1986), pp. 260–61.

7 Chunyi Li, paper summarizing work carried out for AgResearch New Zealand given at World Deer Farming Congress, Changchun, 2010 (unpublished).

8 R. G. Marburger, R. M. Robinson, J. W. Thomas, M. J. Andregg and K. A. Clark, 'Antler Malformation Produced by Leg Injury in White-tailed Deer', *Journal of Wildlife Diseases*, VIII (1972), p. 311.

9 G. B. Wislocki and M. Singer, 'The Occurrence and Function of Nerves in the Growing Antlers of Deer', *Journal of Comparative Neurology*, LXXXV (1946), p. 1.

10 R. V. Short and M. F. Hay, 'Delayed Implantation in the Roe

Deer', *Symposia of the Zoological Society, London*, XV (1966), p. 173.
11 Geist, *Deer of the World*.
12 R. R. Hofmann and D. R. Stewart, 'Grazer or Browser? A
   Classification Based on Stomach Structure and Feeding Habits of
   East African Ruminants', *Mammalia*, XXXVI (1972), pp. 226–40.

3 THE EXPLOITATION OF DEER

1 For more discussion of this subject see John Fletcher, *Fletcher's
   Game: A Vet's Life with Scotland's Deer* (Edinburgh, 2003), and
   Gardens of Earthly Delight: The History of Deer Parks (Oxford, 2011).
2 Marco Masseti, 'Holocene and Anthropochorous Wild Mammals
   of the Mediterranean Islands', *Anthropozoologica*, XXVIII (1998),
   pp. 3–20; Jacqui Mulville, 'Red Deer on Scottish Islands', in
   The Extinct and Introduced Fauna of Britain, 3000BC–AD130,
   ed. T. O'Connor and N. Sykes (Oxford, 2010).
3 Valerius Geist, *Deer of the World: Their Evolution, Behavior and
   Ecology* (Shrewsbury, 1999).
4 G. Kenneth Whitehead, *Encyclopedia of Deer* (Shrewsbury, 1993).
5 Geist, *Deer of the World*.
6 Frederick E. Zeuner, *A History of Domesticated Animals* (London,
   1963).
7 Whitehead, *Encyclopedia of Deer*.
8 Geist, *Deer of the World*.
9 Naomi J. Sykes, Judith White, Tina E. Hayes and Martin R.
   Palmer, 'Tracking Animals Using Strontium Isotopes in Teeth:
   The Role of Fallow Deer (*Dama dama*) in Roman Britain',
   Antiquity, LXXX (2006), pp. 948–59.
10 Gunter Reinken, 'Weider-Verbreitung. Verwendung und
   Namensgebung des Damhirsches Cervus dama L. in Europa',
   Zeitschrift der Jagdwissenschaft, XLIII (1997), pp. 197–206.
11 Donald and Norma Chapman, *Fallow Deer* (Lavenham, 1975).
12 Fletcher, *Gardens of Earthly Delight*.
13 Ibid.
14 Michael Baxter Brown, *Richmond Park: The History of a Royal Deer*

Park (London, 1985).

15 Celia Fiennes, *The Journeys of Celia Fiennes, 1696*, ed. Christopher Morris (London, 1947).

16 These ideas are expanded in Fletcher, *Gardens of Earthly Delight*.

17 Ibid.

18 Jean-Denis Vigne, 'Domestication ou appropriation pour la chasse: histoire d'un choix socio-culturel depuis le Neolithique. L'exemple des cerfs (*Cervus*)', in *Exploitation des Animaux Sauvages à Travers le Temps, XIIIe Rencontres Internationales d'Archéologie et d'Histoire d'Antibes IVe Colloque international de l'Homme et l'Animal*, Société de Recherche Interdisciplinaire (Juan-les-Pins, 1993).

19 John Fletcher, 'The Significance of Samuel Pepys' Predilection for Venison Pasty', *Proceedings of the 2004 Oxford symposium on Food and Cookery* (Totnes, 2004).

20 E. P. Thompson, *Whigs and Hunters: The Origin of the Black Act* (London, 1975).

4 DEER HUNTING AND ART

1 Thomas T. Allsen, *The Royal Hunt in Eurasian History* (Philadelphia, PA, 2006).

2 Diarmuid A. Ó Drisceóil, 'Fulachta Fiadh: The Value of Early Irish Literature', in *Burnt Offerings: International Contributions to Burnt Mound Archaeology*, ed. Victor Buckley (Dublin, 1990).

3 G. Kenneth Whitehead, *Hunting and Stalking Deer in Britain through the Ages* (London, 1980).

4 Joan Aruz, Ann Farkas and Elisabetta Valtz Fino, eds, *The Golden Deer of Eurasia: Perspectives on the Steppe Nomads of the Ancient World*, exh. cat., Metropolitan Museum of Art, New York (2006).

5 Ibid.

6 F.W.M. Vera, *Grazing Ecology and Forest History* (Wallingford, Oxfordshire, 2000).

7 J. K. Anderson, *Hunting in the Ancient World* (Berkeley, 1985).

8 P. B. Munsche, *Gentlemen and Poachers: The English Game Laws,*

1671–1831 (Cambridge, 1981).

9 Jean Birrell, 'Peasant Deer Poachers in the Medieval Forest', in *Progress and Problems in Medieval England*, ed. Richard Britnell and John Hatcher (Cambridge, 1996) pp. 68–89.

10 E. P. Thompson, *Whigs and Hunters: The Origin of the Black Act* (London, 1975).

11 G. Kenneth Whitehead, *Encyclopedia of Deer* (Shrewsbury, 1993).

12 Allsen, *The Royal Hunt in Eurasian History*.

13 Michael Bath, *The Image of the Stag* (Baden-Baden, 1992).

14 Kurt G. Blüchel, *Game and Hunting* (Köln, 1997).

15 G. Kenneth Whitehead, *Hunting and Stalking Deer in Britain through the Ages* (London, 1980).

16 Duff Hart-Davis, *Monarchs of the Glen: A History of Deer-Stalking in the Scottish Highlands* (London, 1978).

5 DEER AS SYMBOLS

Throughout this chapter I have drawn almost exclusively on Michael Bath's *The Image of the Stag* (Baden-Baden, 1992), which treats of the symbolism of deer in greater depth than any other source I have come across.

I have also been influenced by Marcelle Thiébaux's *The Stag of Love: The Chase in Medieval Literature* (Ithaca, NY, 1974).

1 Bath, *The Image of the Stag*.

2 John Cummins, *The Hound and the Hawk: The Art of Medieval Hunting* (London, 1988).

3 The following three papers relate to the strange antlered Chinese tomb guardians: Alfred Salmony, 'Antler and Tongue: An Essay on Ancient Chinese Symbolism and its Implications', *Artibus Asiae supplementum*, XIII (1954); Colin Mackenzie, 'Meaning and Style in the Art of Chu', in *The Problem of Meaning in Early Chinese Ritual Bronzes*, ed. Roderick Whitfield. Percival David Foundation of Chinese Art, *Colloquies on Art and Archaeology in Asia*, XV (1993); Gilles Beguin, *Art Chinois Musée Cernuschi: Acquisitions, 1993–2004*, exh.cat., Musées de la ville de Paris (2005).

4 Michael J. Enright, *The Sutton Hoo Sceptre and the Roots of Celtic Kingship Theory* (Dublin, 2006).

5 Bath, *The Image of the Stag*.

6 Richard Foster, *Patterns of Thought: The Hidden Meaning of the Great Pavement of Westminster Abbey* (London, 1991).

7 Bath, *The Image of the Stag*.

8 Ibid.

9 Ibid.

10 Ibid.

11 Ibid.

12 Ibid.

13 Ibid.

14 Ibid.

15 Ibid.

16 G. Kenneth Whitehead, *Encyclopedia of Deer* (Shrewsbury, 1993).

17 Bath, *The Image of the Stag*.

18 Ibid.

6 DEER IN NORTH AMERICA

1 Valerius Geist, *Deer of the World: Their Evolution, Behavior and Ecology* (Shrewsbury, 1999).

2 Ibid.

3 Richard Nelson, *Heart and Blood: Living with Deer in America* (New York, 1997).

4 Ibid.

5 Ibid.

6 Samuel Merrill, *The Moose Book* (New York, 1916).

7 Nelson, *Heart and Blood*.

8 Ibid.

9 Ibid.

10 Robert Wegner, *Legendary Deer Slayers* (Iola, WI, 2004).

11 Ibid.

12 Ibid.

13 John Fletcher, *Gardens of Earthly Delight: The History of Deer Parks*

(Oxford, 2011).

14 Wegner, *Legendary Deer Slayers*.

15 Ibid.

16 James A. Swan, cited in Foreword, ibid.

17 Matt Cartmill, *A View to a Death in the Morning* (Cambridge, MA, 1993).

18 Geist, *Deer of the World*.

19 Wegner, *Legendary Deer Slayers*.

20 Ibid.

21 Nelson, *Heart and Blood*.

22 Ibid.

23 Oostvaardersplassen, *Report of the International Committee on the Management of large Herbivores in the Oostvaardersplassen* (Lelystad, 2006) Also available at http://www.wing.wur.nl/icmo, accessed 1 August 2012.

24 Nelson, *Heart and Blood*.

7   DEER AND PEOPLE TODAY

1 Jean Birrell, 'Peasant Deer Poachers in the Medieval Forest', in *Progress and Problems in Medieval England*, ed. Richard Britnell and John Hatcher (Cambridge, 1996).

2 G. Kenneth Whitehead, *Deer and their Management in the Deer Parks of Great Britain and Ireland* (London, 1950), and *Hunting and Stalking Deer in Britain through the Ages* (London, 1980).

3 Magnus Magnusson, *Rum: Nature's Island* (Edinburgh, 1998).

4 John Fletcher, *Gardens of Earthly Delight: The History of Deer Parks* (Oxford, 2011).

5 Rory Putman, Marco Apollonio and Reidar Andersen, eds, *Ungulate Management in Europe: Problems and Practices* (Cambridge, 2011).

6 John Fletcher, *Fletcher's Game: A Vet's Life with Scotland's Deer* (Edinburgh, 2003).

7 Deer Industry New Zealand website: www.deernz.org, accessed 1 August 2012.

8 K. L. Blaxter, R.N.B. Kay, G.A.M. Sharman, J.M.M. Cunningham and W. J. Hamilton, *Farming the Red Deer: The First Report of an Investigation by the Rowett Research Institute and the Hill Farming Research Organisation* (Edinburgh, 1974).

9 W. Chan, J. Brown, S. M. Lee and D. H. Buss, *Meat Poultry and Game*, 5th supplement to *McCance and Widdowson's The Composition of Foods* (London, 1995).

10 Michael Crawford and David Marsh, *The Driving Force: Food in Evolution and the Future* (London, 1989).

11 Internet Movie Database (IMDb) www.imdb.com

Select Bibliography

Allsen, Thomas T., *The Royal Hunt in Eurasian History* (Philadelphia, PA, 2006)

Anderson, J. K., *Hunting in the Ancient World* (Berkeley, CA, 1985)

Aruz, Joan, Ann Farkas and Elisabetta Valtz Fino, eds, *The Golden Deer of Eurasia: Perspectives on the Steppe Nomads of the Ancient World*, exh. cat., Metropolitan Museum of Art (New York, 2006)

Bath, Michael, *The Image of the Stag* (Baden-Baden, 1992)

Baxter Brown, Michael, *Richmond Park: The History of a Royal Deer Park* (London, 1985)

Beguin, Gilles, *Art Chinois Musée Cernuschi, Acquisitions, 1993–2004*, exh. cat., Musées de la ville de Paris (Paris, 2005)

Birrell, Jean, 'Peasant Deer Poachers in the Medieval Forest', in *Progress and Problems in Medieval England*, ed. Richard Britnell and John Hatcher (Cambridge, 1996), pp. 68–89

Blaxter, K. L., R.N.B. Kay, G.A.M. Sharman, J.M.M. Cunningham and W. J. Hamilton, *Farming the Red Deer: The First Report of an Investigation by the Rowett Research Institute and the Hill Farming Research Organisation* (Edinburgh, 1974)

Blüchel, Kurt G., *Game and Hunting* (Köln, 1997)

Cartmill, Matt, *A View to a Death in the Morning* (Harvard, MA, 1993)

Chan, W., J. Brown, S. M. Lee and D. H. Buss, 'Meat Poultry and Game', 5th supplement to *McCance and Widdowson's The Composition of Foods* (London, 1995)

Chapman, Donald, and Norma Chapman, *Fallow Deer* (Lavenham, 1975)

Chapman, N. G., and S. Harris, *Muntjac* (Fordingbridge and London, 1996)

Clutton-Brock, T. H., and S. D. Albon, *Red Deer in the Highlands* (London, 1989)

Crawford, Michael, and David Marsh, *The Driving Force: Food in Evolution and the Future* (London, 1989)

Cummins, John, *The Hound and the Hawk: The Art of Medieval Hunting* (London, 1988)

Darwall, G.H.D., and R. G. Clark, 'On the Growth and Form of Deer Antlers', *Deer*, VI (1986), pp. 260–61

Enright, Michael J., *The Sutton Hoo Sceptre and the Roots of Celtic Kingship Theory* (Dublin, 2006)

Fiennes, Celia, *The Journeys of Celia Fiennes, 1696*, ed. Christopher Morris (London, 1947)

Fletcher, John, *Fletcher's Game: A Vet's Life with Scotland's Deer* (Edinburgh, 2003)

—, 'The Significance of Samuel Pepys' Predilection for Venison Pasty', *Proceedings of the 2004 Oxford Symposium on Food and Cookery* (Totnes, 2004), pp. 23–35

—, *Gardens of Earthly Delight: The History of Deer Parks* (Oxford, 2011)

Foster, Richard, *Patterns of Thought: The Hidden Meaning of the Great Pavement of Westminster Abbey* (London, 1991)

Geist, Valerius, *Deer of the World: Their Evolution, Behavior and Ecology* (Shrewsbury, 1999)

Gilbert, Clément, Anne Ropiquet and Alexandre Hassanin, 'Mitochondrial and Nuclear Phylogenies of Cervidae (Mammalia, Ruminantia): Systematics, Morphology and Biogeography', *Molecular Phylogenetics and Evolution*, XL (2006), pp. 101–17

Grubb, P., 'Order Artiodactyla', in *Mammal Species of the World: A Taxonomic and Geographic Reference*, ed. Don E. Wilson and DeeAnn M. Reeder (Washington, DC, and London, 1993), pp. 384–92

Hart-Davis, Duff, *Monarchs of the Glen: A History of Deer-stalking in the Scottish Highlands* (London, 1978)

Hofmann, R. R., and D. R. Stewart, 'Grazer or Browser? A Classification Based on Stomach Structure and Feeding Habits of East African Ruminants', *Mammalia*, XXXVI (1972), pp. 226–40

Langbein, Jochen, *Ungulate Management in Europe: Problems and Practices*, ed. Rory Putman, Marco Apollonio and Reidar Andersen (Cambridge, 2011)

Li, Chunyi, 'Paper Summarising Work Carried Out for AgResearch New Zealand given at World Deer Farming Congress, Changchun', 2010 (unpublished)

Lister, A. M., C. J. Edwards, D.A.W. Nock, M. Bruce, I. A. van Pijlen, D. G. Bradley, M. G. Thomas and I. Barnes, 'The Phylogenetic Position of the "Giant Deer" *Megaloceros giganteus*', *Nature*, CDXXXVIII (2005), pp. 850–53

Mackenzie, Colin, 'Meaning and Style in the Art of Chu', in *The Problem of Meaning in Early Chinese Ritual Bronzes*, ed. Roderick Whitfield, Colloquies on Art and Archaeology in Asia, 15 (London, 1993)

Magnusson, Magnus, *Rum: Nature's Island* (Edinburgh, 1998)

Marburger, R. G., R. M. Robinson, J. W. Thomas, M. J. Andregg and K. A. Clark, 'Antler Malformation Produced by Leg Injury in White-tailed Deer', *Journal of Wildlife Disease*, VIII (1972), p. 311

Masseti, Marco, 'Holocene and Anthropochorous Wild Mammals of the Mediterranean Islands', *Anthropozoologica*, XXVIII (1998), pp. 3–20

—, ed. *Island of Deer: Natural History of the Fallow Deer of Rhodes and of the Vertebrates of Dodecanese, Greece* (Rhodes, 2002)

—, Elena Pecchioli, Cristiano Vernesi, 'Phylogeography of the Last Surviving Populations of Rhodian and Anatolian Fallow Deer (*Dama dama dama L.*, 1758)', *Biological Journal of the Linnean Society*, XCIII (2008), pp. 835–44

Merrill, Samuel, *The Moose Book* (New York, 1916)

Mowat, Farley, *People of the Deer* (London, 1954)

Munsche, P. B., *Gentlemen and Poachers: The English Game Laws, 1671–1831* (Cambridge, 1981)

Mulville, Jacqui, 'Red Deer on Scottish Islands', in *The Extinct and Introduced Fauna of Britain, 3000 BC–130 AD*, ed. T. O'Connor and N. Sykes (Oxford, 2010)

Nelson, Richard, *Heart and Blood: Living with Deer in America* (New York, 1997)

Noble, W. C., and Jaqueline E. M. Crerar, 'Management of White-tailed Deer by the Neutral Iroquois, AD 999–1651', *Archaeozoologia*, VI/11 (1993), pp. 19–70

Ó Drisceóil, Diarmuid A., 'Fulachta Fiadh: The Value of Early Irish Literature', in *Burnt Offerings: International Contributions to Burnt Mound Archaeology*, ed. Victor Buckley (Dublin, 1990)

Oostvaardersplassen, *Report of the International Committee on the Management of large Herbivores in the Oostvaardersplassen* (Lelystad, 2006) Also available at www.wing.wur.nl/icmo

Pitra, Christian, Joerns Fickel, Erik Meijaard and P. Colin Groves, 'Evolution and Phylogeny of Old World Deer', *Molecular Phylogenetics and Evolution*, XXXIII (2004), pp. 880–95

Pitts, Michael, and Mark Roberts, *Fairweather Eden: Life in Britain Half a Million Years Ago as Revealed by the Excavations at Boxgrove* (London, 1998)

Putman, Rory, Marco Apollonio and Reidar Andersen, eds, *Ungulate Management in Europe: Problems and Practices* (Cambridge, 2011)

Rawlings, Marjorie Kinnan, *The Yearling* (New York, 1938)

Reinken, Gunter, 'Weider-Verbreitung. Verwendung und Namensgebung des Damhirsches Cervus dama L. in Europa', *Zeitschrift der Jagdwissenschaft*, XLIII (1997), pp. 197–206

Salmony, Alfred, 'Antler and Tongue: An Essay on Ancient Chinese Symbolism and its Implications', *Artibus Asiae supplementum*, XIII (1954)

Short, R. V., and M. F. Hay, 'Delayed Implantation in the Roe Deer', *Symposia of the Zoological Society, London*, XV (1966), p. 173

Stephen, Oscar Leslie, *Sir Victor Brooke, Sportsman and Naturalist: A Memoir of his Life and Extracts from his Letters and Journals* (Milton Keynes, n. d. [c. 1891])

Sykes, Naomi J., Judith White, Tina E. Hayes and Martin R. Palmer, 'Tracking Animals Using Strontium Isotopes in Teeth: The Role of Fallow Deer (*Dama dama*) in Roman Britain', *Antiquity*, LXXX (2006), pp. 948–59

—, 'Animal Bones and Animal Parks', in *The Medieval Park: New Perspectives*, ed. R. Liddiard (Cheshire, 2007), pp. 49–62

Thiébaux, Marcelle, *The Stag of Love: The Chase in Medieval Literature* (Cornell, 1974)

Thompson, E. P., *Whigs and Hunters: The Origin of the Black Act* (London, 1975)

Vera, F.W.M., *Grazing Ecology and Forest History* (Wallingford, Oxfordshire, 2000)

Vigne, Jean-Denis, 'Domestication ou appropriation pour la chasse: histoire d'un choix socio-culturel depuis le Neolithique. L'exemple des cerfs (*Cervus*)', in *Exploitation des Animaux Sauvages à Travers le Temps, XIIIe Rencontres Internationales d'Archéologie et d'Histoire d'Antibes IVe Colloque international de l'Homme et l'Animal*, Société de Recherche Interdisciplinaire (Juan-les-Pins, 1993)

Wegner, Robert, *Legendary Deer Slayers* (Iola, WI, 2004)

Whitehead, G. Kenneth, *Deer and their Management in the Deer Parks of Great Britain and Ireland* (London, 1950)

—, *The Deer of Great Britain and Ireland* (London, 1964)

—, *Deer of the World*. Constable (London, 1972)

—, *Hunting and Stalking Deer in Britain through the Ages* (London, 1980)

—, *Encyclopedia of Deer* (Shrewsbury, 1993)

Wislocki, G. B., and M. Singer, 'The Occurrence and Function of Nerves in the Growing Antlers of Deer', *Journal of Comparative Neurology*, LXXXV (1946), p. 1

Yu, Z., 'Development of the Chinese Deer Farming Industry and the Market for Deer Velvet', in *Advances in Antler Science and Product Technology* (2nd International Symposium) (Auckland, 2004), pp. 233–8

Zeuner, Frederick E., *A History of Domesticated Animals* (London, 1963)

Associations and Websites

BRITISH DEER FARMS AND PARKS ASSOCIATION
PO Box 7522
Matlock, DE4 9BR
United Kingdom
www.bdfpa.org

BRITISH DEER SOCIETY
The Walled Garden
Burgate Manor
Fordingbridge, Hampshire SP6 1EF
www.bds.org.uk

DEER INDUSTRY NEW ZEALAND
PO Box 10702
Wellington, 6143
New Zealand
www.deernz.org

SCOTTISH VENISON PARTNERSHIP
www.scottish-venison.info

NORTH AMERICAN DEER FARMERS ASSOCIATION
1428 Market Ave North
Canton, Ohio, 44714
USA
www.nadefa.org

FEDERATION OF EUROPEAN DEER FARMERS' ASSOCIATIONS
http://www.fedfa.org

DEER INITIATIVE
The Carriage House
Brynkinalt Business Centre
Chirk,Wrexham LL14 5NS
www.thedeerinitiative.co.uk

VENISON ADVISORY SERVICE
Winton Loan
Edinburgh EH10 7AN
www.venisonadvisory.com

Acknowledgements

First I wish to thank my wife, Nichola. She has always encouraged me to take time away from Scotland in our little French tower so that I could write this book.

I thank Professor Adrian Lister at the Natural History Museum in London for directing me towards papers by Gilbert and Pitra and colleagues which allowed me to write what is, I hope, a contemporary account of the classification of deer. I also thank those whose books and articles I have plundered, in particular two Scottish academics, Michael Bath and John Cummins, and, in America, Marcelle Thiébaux for her inspirational *The Stag of Love: The Chase in Medieval Literature* and Professor Val Geist who wrote *Deer of the World* and who explained to me the American concept of not trading indigenous wildlife production. George Darwall cheerfully gave me permission to use his theory on antler growth; Professor Jerry Haigh introduced me to the strange tongued tomb guardians of Tang dynasty China.

Norma Chapman, Dr Naomi Sykes, and Professor Marco Masseti have always been encouraging and have shared their infectious passion for fallow deer. Among deer-park keepers I count myself lucky to have met James Ellis, Julian Stoyel and Jeremy Elliott, and among vets Mike Bringans and José Antonio Ortiz who have all made me feel like a young stag again. Many kindly contributed photographs, including Neil Clarke and Bud Graske, while Monica Santos helped me find films with a cervine content. To you all I wish to say thank you.

At Reaktion, Michael Leaman and Jonathan Burt have been patient and helpful, for which I am truly grateful. The concept of the Animal series deserves great credit and I am privileged to have contributed.

Photo Acknowledgements

Images author's collection except for Art Resource, New York: p. 100 (Erich Lessing); Bodleian Library, University of Oxford: pp. 109, 128; Mike Brigans: p. 70; Brooklyn Museum of Art: p. 146; Neil Clarke: p. 51; Clock House Furniture: p. 180; Fine Arts Museums of San Francisco: p. 108 (Gift of Peter F. Young 76.26.19); Nichola Fletcher: p. 118; Bud Graske: p. 131; Library of Congress, Washington, DC: pp. 14, 156, 157, 158; David Mason: p. 71; The Metropolitan Museum of Art, New York: p. 28 (Charles Stewart Smith Collection, Gift of Mrs Charles Stewart Smith, Charles Stewart Smith Jr., and Howard Caswell Smith, in memory of Charles Stewart Smith, 1914 (14.76.61.24); The Minneapolis Institute of Arts: p. 98 (Gift of Mrs C. J. Martin in memory of Charles Jairus Martin 34.4); Shutterstock: p. 10 (Tom Reichner); Julian Soyel: pp. 24, 41, 61; Worcester Art Museum, Massachusetts: p. 159; Zoological Society of London: pp. 18, 21, 26, 34, 68.

Index